What People Are Saying About
55 Ways to Promote & Sell
Your Book on the Internet

"If you want to increase you[r ...] new book. This comprehens[ive] resource will demystify onlin[e ...] rolling. It's just the kick i[n ...] goose your book sales." -[Steve ...] of *Plug Your Book!* and *ePublish*.

"No matter where you are on your publishing journey, Bob Baker's *55 Ways* book is a must-have. In it, he reveals dozens of smart, rock-solid resources you can use today. Bob created a brand new mold — one that is sure to support your success while showing you a great time along the way."
-**Paulette Ensign**, www.TipsBooklets.com

"Bob's book offers wonderful advice for marketing your book online! His message is rich with experience and enthusiasm. *55 Ways* is not weighed down by a lot of hype. It gets straight to the point and readies you for action!" -**Deltina Hay**, author of *A Survival Guide to Social Media and Web 2.0 Optimization*, www.SocialMediaPower.com

"Reading Bob's *55 Ways* book is like having your very own marketing/promotion/communications coach! Bob's conversational style makes his promotional expertise accessible and easy to implement quickly. Bob's track record of success is evident in the variety of ways he uses new media to promote his own work. Now, it's your chance to learn from the best and enjoy success!" -**Maria Rodgers O'Rourke**, author of *Prepare Your Heart for a Great Christmas* and *Prepare Your Heart to Be a Great Mom*

More Praise for *55 Ways* ...

"Being in the book business, I have spent thousands of dollars on marketing — of course, looking for gems like these. You have put them all together in this book. Powerful! I praise you for your insights and generosity in sharing them."
-**Ardy Skinner**, author of *The Lavish Cheapskate*, www.LavishCheapskate.com

"Bob's new book is a lifesaver. His research saves me time. I immediately applied his experience, tips and expertise to my own promotion efforts."
-**Larry De Rusha**, author of *The Secret of Knowing* and *Romancing the Divine*, www.LarryDeRusha.com

"Bob's new book is an essential reference for any writer or creative person, no matter how much of a beginner or expert they are. Priced right too. Section 3, 'Promoting Your Book Across the Internet,' contains exceptional advice for anyone marketing anything online — books, music, crafts, events, or services. Well done!" -**John Willmott**, Celtic Ways, www.celticways.com

"I've been reading Bob's work ever since *Branding Yourself Online*. This book, like all his others, is simple, straight-forward, concise and chock-full of information. *55 Ways* is easy to follow and guides you step by step through an otherwise overwhelming subject matter. I recommend Bob's work to many of my clients. This one will definitely be on the recommended reading list." -**Philip Horvath**, transformational catalyst and co-founder of c3: Center for Conscious Creativity

55 Ways to Promote & Sell Your Book on the Internet

Bob Baker

Jim,
Get out there
and promote
yourself!

FullTimeAuthor.com
St. Louis, MO

55 Ways to Promote & Sell Your Book on the Internet

Published by Spotlight Publications and FullTimeAuthor.com
PO Box 43058, St. Louis, MO 63143 USA
(314) 963-5296 • bob@bob-baker.com

ISBN-10: 0-9714838-6-8
ISBN-13: 978-0-9714838-6-6

Printed in the United States of America.

Disclaimer

This book is designed to provide information on marketing, promoting, and selling books. It is sold with the understanding that the publisher and author are not engaged in rendering legal, accounting, or other professional services. If legal or other expert assistance is required, the services of a competent professional should be sought.

It is not the purpose of this book to cover the full range of information that is otherwise available on this topic, but instead to complement, amplify, and supplement other texts. You are urged to read all available material and tailor the information to your individual needs.

Every effort has been made to make this book as accurate as possible. However, there may be mistakes, and with all the rapid changes online, some details may be inaccurate by the time you read this. Therefore, this text should be used only as a general guide and not as the ultimate source of information on the topic.

The author and publisher shall have neither liability nor responsibility to any person or entity with respect to any loss or damage caused, or alleged to have been caused, directly or indirectly, by the information contained in this book.

To Kelli and Pooki

Acknowledgements

So many people come to mind as I think of those who encouraged and inspired me to write this book. First, I thank my friends and colleagues at the St. Louis Publishers Association (including Sue, Ed, Christine, Barbara, Lynnette, Bill, Linda, Natasha, Sue W, Ligaya, Bobette, and Andy) who repeatedly demonstrated their faith in me to deliver advice and inspiration to our members.

Thanks to Robin Bartlett, Terry Nathan, Lisa Krebs Magno, Florrie Binford Kichler, and Teresa Fogarty from the Independent Book Publishers Association. Thanks also to the many cool friends I now have in the book world, including Kathleen Gage, Paulette Ensign, Penny Sansevieri, Steve O'Keefe, Brian Judd, Shel Horowitz, David Mathison, Andrew Chapman, Peter Bowerman, Bob Goodman, Tami Dever, Steve Weber, Deltina Hay, and Sharon Castlen.

I especially appreciate my close circle of creative friends: Scott Ginsberg, Joan Marie, George Dewey Hinds, Maria Rogers O'Rourke, and Lee Mueller — as well as my mastermind pals Steve O'Rourke, Toni McMurphy, and Cynde Meyer. Thanks to Corrine Richardson, Bobbi Linkemer, and others who gave me great feedback on the early drafts of the *55 Ways* book and web site.

A big tip of my cap to self-publishing and book marketing trailblazers Dan Poynter and John Kremer!

Most importantly, I want to express deep gratitude to my radiant soul mate Pooki and my beautiful daughter Kelli. They support and inspire me with their unconditional love! I dedicate this book to them.

About the Author

Bob Baker is a full-time author and independent publisher who has developed a successful niche writing and speaking about music marketing and self-promotion for songwriters, musicians and bands. His books include *Guerrilla Music Marketing Handbook*, *Unleash the Artist Within*, *Branding Yourself Online*, and more.

Since 1995 Bob has published *The Buzz Factor* ezine, one of the first music tips email newsletters in existence. In the many years since, he has used the Internet almost exclusively to spread his message and promote and sell his books.

He served three terms as president of the St. Louis Publishers Association, is a regular presenter at IBPA's Publishing University, and is an advocate for the independent publishing movement.

Bob is also an active speaker, blogger and podcaster who is passionate about showing creative people how to make the most of their talents using the Internet and low-cost guerrilla marketing tactics.

Visit TheBuzzFactor.com and FullTimeAuthor.com for more details.

Contents

This Is Just the Beginning of Your Book Promotion Journey

You are about to embark on an exciting Internet book promotion adventure. No doubt, there's work to be done and there will be challenges ahead, but the potential rewards that lie before you just may exceed your greatest expectations.

But to enjoy the rewards you must be vigilant in the pursuit of your book publishing goals. You must stay focused and regularly feed your mind with new ideas and fresh perspectives on marketing. That's why I encourage you to think of this book as an important first step in your journey.

I invite you to stay in touch with me and report your progress. So before you continue reading, please visit my web site at **FullTimeAuthor.com** and download a copy of *Self-Publishing Confidential*, a free report filled with my best book publishing and marketing advice. And while you're there, sign up for my free *Full-Time Author* ezine.

Also, send me a friend invite on Facebook at **Facebook.com/BobBaker** and follow me on Twitter at **Twitter.com/MrBuzzFactor**.

At the very end of the book, I'll issue a "55 Ways Internet Book Promotion Challenge" and invite you to join a special Facebook group of other authors on this same journey. *To your success!*

–Bob

Introduction

The Internet. It's huge — and growing all the time. And the really great thing is that millions of people go online every day to search for and purchase books.

Let's take a quick look at the book slice of the online pie:

- According to Nielsen Online, more books are sold on the Internet than any other product. And the numbers are increasing: 41% of Internet users purchased books online in 2008, up from 34% two years earlier.

- Amazon.com sold more than $5.3 billion worth of books, music and DVDs in 2008. On average, Amazon sells between 150,000 and 200,000 different book titles every day.

- Barnes & Noble's web site rang up $466 million in sales in 2008.

- Ebook sales worldwide were $323 million in 2008 and are expected to grow to nearly $9 billion by 2013 (according to research firm In-Stat).

No doubt, there's a lot of book buying and selling going on in cyberspace.

Now for the bad news ...

The Internet can seem overwhelming and mysterious to a lot of people — including tech-savvy authors and publishers. There are so many options ...

and only so much time and money to invest in it.

Perspective: Don't be intimidated. You don't have to compete with the big players to be successful. Just take it one step at a time. That's what I did. And that approach has served me well.

My Journey to Full-Time Author Status

In 1987 I began publishing a music magazine in St. Louis, MO. A couple of years later I started writing a monthly column that offered tips on how to build a successful music career. My musician readers raved about it, which encouraged me to write more.

In 1996, I took more than a dozen of the best columns and compiled them into a book I called the *Guerrilla Music Marketing Handbook*.

I had little knowledge of the book publishing business and, frankly, had no interest in putting together a book proposal, seeking out a literary agent, or enduring a parade of rejection letters from publishing companies. So, I decided to put out the book myself.

It wasn't pretty. The first edition was published in an unimpressive-looking, bare-bones, three-ring binder. At first, I averaged only a few sales per month, but the response from readers was immediately favorable.

The *Guerrilla Music Marketing Handbook* was one of the early titles that didn't focus on "how to get a record deal" and instead encouraged artists to take a more creative, hands-on approach to marketing and career development.

Taking the Unconventional Path

When it came to promoting the book, I practiced what I preached and steered clear of many traditional steps. For one, I never pursued retail distribution in bookstores — something most authors consider to be a requirement.

Instead, I decided to use the Internet as my primary exposure and sales tool. My goal was to bypass the standard channels and take my message directly to the people who needed to hear it the most: readers and buyers.

I also wasn't concerned with making a big splash with the "launch" of the *Guerrilla Music Marketing Handbook*. Book publishers typically allot a two- to four-month window during which they heavily promote a new title (similar to how record labels and movie studios handle new releases). The idea is to strike while a book is still considered "fresh."

I, on the other hand, took a long-term approach. I started small and watched the book's popularity slowly grow over the ensuing decade. Every couple of years, I added to and updated the chapters, improved the format and design, and continued to get the word out via the Internet and periodic speaking events.

Results: Over the years the book has seemingly taken on a life of its own. Through word-of-mouth recommendations, magazine reviews, widespread exposure on the Internet, and nice perks like a cameo in the movie *The School of Rock* ... the *Guerrilla Music* book has become my best-selling title and is largely responsible for me living my dream of being a full-time author. And there's no sign of the buzz slowing down — sales continue to grow every year.

That one book lead to five more paperback books, as well as an entire line of info-products and services geared toward musicians, authors, and other creative people: ebooks, special reports, audio programs, consulting work, and more.

Benefits: Because of the strong presence and reputation I've built on the Internet over the years, new opportunites come my way all the time. In 2007, I developed an online music marketing course for Berklee College of Music and am now part of Berklee's online faculty.

In addition, I am often invited to speak at music and book conferences all over the world. Plus, I've gotten my fair share of media exposure on NPR and several national magazines — all because of what I've done online.

Yes, I've had to work day jobs here and there over the years to make ends meet. But in 2003, I put in my notice to quit the last job I ever plan to work for someone else. That feeling of independence is price-less. Through this book and my FullTimeAuthor.com web site, I hope to inspire you and countless others to enjoy that same level of satisfaction.

Making smart and consistent use of the Internet has been very good for my career as an author. And I'm convinced that it can be very good for you too.

An Important Thing to Note

In this book I share the 55 best ways I've found to promote myself and my books online. But you don't have to implement all of these ideas and take all the steps I've taken to be successful. In fact, you shouldn't even try. The worst thing you can do is flip through these pages, declare "There's no way I can do all this stuff and still have a life," and end up doing nothing.

Think of this as an all-you-can-eat buffet. Sure, you could eat some of everything that's laid out before you. But you shouldn't do that. If you did, you'd stuff yourself and feel bloated and uncomfortable.

Instead, look over what's available to you and make choices. "Oh, I like that. That looks good too. I've never tried that before, but it seems like it might be fun to sample."

Best approach: Ease into this Internet marketing thing. Look over the simple ideas in this book and see what catches your eye. What resonates with you? Try out a couple of new online tactics first, then a few more. Also, look over the suggested steps I outline in the "Final Thoughts" section at the end of this book.

Before you know it, you'll be creating a buzz and attracting attention to your book and to yourself online. Your friends will be amazed. And your growing number of dedicated readers (and buyers) will love you for it.

Are you ready to get started?

Good. Let's dive in!

Section One

Laying the Foundation for Online Book Promotion

1

Understand the 3 Steps to Effective Book Promotion

Here's a simple question for you:

What is book marketing?

Sure, you know it's something you have to do. You have at least some grasp of what is it. You recognize it when you see it (most of the time). But at its most basic level, can you explain what it is?

And more importantly, can you spell out the basic elements of effective book marketing? Because, after all, if you're going to invest your time and energy in Internet promotion, it better be effective. Right?

Don't worry if you don't have a quick answer to my question. On the other hand, please don't curse me if you think you know the answer and feel my probing here is pointless. Because it isn't.

Key: If you plan to read this book and use these ideas to create a book promotion plan, you need to understand the underlying principles at work here. These elements are simple, but they're often glossed over by eager authors and publishers who just want to "get their name out there."

Getting your name out there is fine. It's better than doing nothing at all. But mindless book marketing — without focus and purpose — usually leads to frustration and continued obscurity.

The solution: Look under the hood and get a grasp of what's at the core of every effective book promotion plan.

The Three Stages of Book Marketing

When it comes right down to it, online book promotion consists of these three elements:

1) Creating awareness — taking action to communicate your identity to a specific audience

2) Making connections — starting and maintaining relationships with a growing number of fans and media/business contacts

3) Asking for the sale — generating cash flow and creating incentives for fans to spend money

There they are: The three stages of marketing. In a nutshell.

Seems simple enough, right? Then why do so many book promoters get it wrong? They spend time on one or two of these stages but ignore the second or third. Or they get busy doing a bunch of marketing "stuff" but don't stop and think long enough to ponder how their efforts fit into the three-stage process.

Want some examples?

Have you ever seen an author or book publisher run an ad that shouts out something along the lines of "*Wakeup Call*, the New Book from Jeff Johnson and Baracuda Publishing. In Stores Now!"

That's it. Just the name of the book, the author, and the publisher ... and the fact that it is now on sale. Perhaps you've even created an ad, flier or web site like this yourself.

Question: What's wrong with this picture? Well, with this approach, the ad is creating awareness, and it does ask for the sale. But it leaves out an entire, all-important stage: developing relationships with fans.

This error would be especially unforgivable if this was the only marketing method the author was using. Why? Because consumers typically need repeated exposures to something before they'll get out their wallets. In addition, they need to feel a connection to the book and the author. This announcment does nothing to facilitate the relationship. And that means wasted time and money spent on promotion.

Way too many aspiring authors skip over this crucial "making connections" step. And they do so at their own peril. Usually, authors don't even realize they're turning their backs on this concept, or they don't comprehend the importance of it to begin with.

Core idea: As a self-promoting author, you can't think only in terms of marketing to the masses. That's an outdated, traditional strategy. So stop thinking about marketing as a way to catapult your message to an enormous, faceless crowd from a distance.

Internet book promotion, when done right, is personal. It's often delivered one-on-one. And even when you do direct a message to a sizeable audience, that audience should ideally be targeted and pre-disposed to like you. And, when communicating to crowds, your tone must be warm and personal.

In fact, this is a great way to set yourself apart from other authors who are mass-promoted and "handled" by corporations. So put a priority on being accessible and establishing relationships with your readers.

Another example: Have you ever known (or seen in the mirror) a gifted author who produced a masterful book filled with ideas that thousands of people need to hear? He or she may even have a sparkling personality and a talent for connecting with people face to face.

But ... they drop the ball when it comes to asking for the sale and generating cash flow. They don't make people aware that they even have books for sale and don't make enticing offers for potential fans to buy now.

Again, they're only putting together pieces of the marketing puzzle. And it's the missing pieces that are stopping them from reaching the significant author status they truly deserve.

So commit these three simple steps to memory. Engrave them in your brain. And as you create your new Internet book promotion plan, make sure your efforts are hitting on a solid combination of these three effective marketing steps:

- **Creating awareness**
- **Making connections**
- **Asking for the sale**

Keeping your eye on these simple elements will make a world of difference in your pursuit of book publishing success.

#2
Develop a Web "Presence" — Not Just a Web Site

When many novice promoters think of Internet marketing, they believe it's all about putting up a good web site and then driving traffic to it using banner ads or a Google AdWords campaign (more on these later).

Sure, that's one way to promote your books online. But it's one of the least effective, in my opinion.

Another line of faulty reasoning is thinking that online book promotion is about search engine optimization (SEO). If only you did well in search results, you're worries would be over. It's true that putting basic SEO principles into practice can be helpful. But it's still not the ultimate solution.

Key: The best way to promote and sell your books online — based on my many years of Internet experience — is thinking outside your web site.

Make no mistake, you need an attractive and well-organized site (and I'll cover my top tips in that area soon). But to make a real impact as an author, you need much more than a good web site.

You Need a Web Presence!

But what do I mean by "presence"?

You have a strong presence online when a growing

number of people who have an interest in your topic or genre keep finding you in the places where they spend time online.

Sure, doing well in Google searches for your ideal words and phrases is one important part of having an Internet presence. But there's so much more to it.

Having a Web presence also means that your articles and sample chapters appear on prominent sites that cater to your subject matter. It means your name keeps popping up on active discussion forums related to your topic.

You also expand your presence when people find you on Facebook, Twitter, YouTube, LinkedIn, and any number of other social networking sites. It grows when people who subscribe to your email newsletter forward your latest message to their friends.

You further establish your presence by starting your own blog, while also making comments on other people's blogs and podcasts. It expands again when you do text, audio and video interviews online.

Bottom line: You set yourself up for success by making sure you can be found in multiple places where your ideal reader, buyer and fan hangs out online.

That's what I mean by developing a Web presence. And that's exactly what this book will help you do.

3

Think Narrow, Not Wide

It's a big world out there — especially on the Internet. The number of Internet users worldwide now exceeds 1.5 billion people.

That's right. Billion with a B.

More than 250 million of those users are in North America alone. It's intimidating to think about connecting with all those people. No wonder so many authors get frustrated and feel overwhelmed when it comes to promoting themselves online.

Have no fear. You don't have to reach all those people. You don't even have to reach all book lovers online. If you try, you'll never reach your goals and will curse me and anyone who's ever been associated with the Internet — including Al Gore.

Key insight: To successfully promote your book, you need to start a relationship with only a small sliver of the total number of people online.

Think about these numbers: If you could reach just one-hundredth of one percent of those 1.5 billion people, you'd have 150,000 potential buyers and fans. That's a lot of people!

Consider my own position in the book publishing world. I am not a best-selling author in the traditional, *New York Times* bestseller list mode of defining success. I am not a household name. Far from it.

Most people have never heard of me and never will.

I am not famous by all the old standards. But I am fairly well-known to a select group of people: primarily, independent musicans. As of this writing, I have more than 15,000 people in my database — a combination of paying customers and people who subscribe to my various free email lists.

Among these people you'll find everything from casual readers to hardcore fans. The numbers aren't staggering by "industry" standards, but they are plenty big enough to allow me to make a living doing something I love.

Conclusion: Don't try to be all things to all people. Don't attempt to reach a wide section of the online population. It's not all about huge numbers.

Your objective is to focus your limited time and energy on the web sites, ezines, and online forums where the people most likely to be attracted to your book hang out.

That's it.

Got it? Good.

#4
Focus on the Most Important Success Factor

Authors venture onto the Web for all sorts of reasons. Some put up a web site just because everybody else is doing it or because they think it's the best way to impress "industry people." Others establish an Internet presence because they think search engines will list their site and drive traffic to it while they sleep.

What's the real reason you should promote your book online? Here's my best answer, and you should apply this concept to just about every action you take to promote yourself, online and off:

Your main focus should be to attract your ideal reader while nurturing relationships with a growing number of fans.

No other factor will influence your level of success like a large and enthusiastic fan base.

It doesn't matter how impressive your publishing company, attorney, agent, publicist, or sales rep is. None of that means squat if fans don't connect with you and your book. However, you can have no publisher, attorney, agent, etc., and still be a huge success if you have fans — and lots of them.

Fans are the only thing that counts (along with the quality of your book and your integrity), so put a priority on courting them. Use the unique interactive qualities of the Web to communicate with people interested in your book topic. Get to know them. Allow them to get to know you and the intimate details that led you to create the book they enjoy so much.

Some authors and publishers refer to this coveted group of people as customers, readers, consumers, clients, or buyers. I prefer to call them ...

FANS!

Readers and buyers will consume your words and purchase your titles. Customers and clients are good for your book business. But *fans* will catapult you into the success stratosphere!

Fans rave about you and help create that priceless "word of mouth" buzz. Your biggest fans will buy practically everything you publish and will drive for hours to hear you speak. In essence, fans are your greatest supporters. And the more of them you have, the more your impact and income will grow.

Insight: The funny thing is, all those "book industry" entities (retail stores, libraries, distributors, media) that ignore you when you're just starting out ... They all become much more interested in you when you have lots of fans.

So forget all the hype and distractions and put your focus where it needs to be the most:

On cultivating fans!

#5
Know Who Your Ideal Fan Is

Could you sit down right now and write a profile of your ideal fan? Can you articulate how your fans dress, where they work, what TV shows they watch, which blogs they read, what they do for fun, what causes they support, and who their favorite cultural hero is?

If you can't describe your fans in detail, you should immediately start searching for a way to do so. Knowing precisely who your fans are dictates what avenues you use to reach them and how you communicate your message once you do reach them.

Reality: Continuing to ignore these insights will lead to missed opportunities and wasted time. If you don't know where your fans hang out, what they're interested in, and why they spend money ... how will you ever be able to effectively promote yourself and your book online?

When you overlook this element, potential fans move on without the benefit of your words and ideas. And you stumble on without the satisfaction of having shared your message and getting the recognition and income that come with it.

The solution: Do some basic, informal research. If you speak in public at all, start asking questions of the people in the crowd during breaks and after your talks. Write down your observations. What types of people come to see you? What traits do your fans have in common? Asking questions may even allow you to discover a segment of the population you've been ignoring but might benefit from your books.

For instance, my books are primarily aimed at self-promoting musicians, songwriters and bands. But early on I discovered they were also being read by artist managers, publicists, booking agents, and even music event and venue managers. Knowing this opened up several new avenues through which I could spread my message of "guerrilla music marketing."

If you're just starting out, observe the types of people who patronize similar authors. Or simply describe the type of person to whom you want your book to appeal.

Helpful tip: If you're really stumped, take a look in the mirror. Since your book is a reflection of you, most likely it appeals to other people just like you. So ... who are you? Where do *you* hang out online and off? How do *you* find out about new books and authors? Your answers contain valuable clues.

This doesn't have to be a complicated research project. Just get a solid handle on the types of people you want to reach with your online promotion and sales messages.

Doing so will help you get to them faster.

#6
Create a Brand Identity Statement

Imagine that your book is the steel tip of a dart. Now visualize that the people of the world are spread out across a giant wall filled with thousands of dartboards. Each dartboard represents a specific demographic group.

For instance, one might be teenagers who like science fiction while another symbolizes adults who enjoy lighthearted mysteries. Other dartboards might represent people who enjoy books about spirituality, health and fitness, history, self-help, software applications, and so on.

Key insight: When you market your books, your job is to aim the tip of your dart directly at the bull's-eye of the dartboards that exemplify your ideal fans. You do this by sending targeted messages to the web sites, blogs, podcasts, online forums, and ezines used by the types of people most likely to be interested in your book's subject matter.

That's the whole point of all this introspective research. Once you know who you're ideal fans are, you can determine what online destinations they patronize. Then send focused messages through those channels.

But what kind of messages do you send? Most

27

authors who market their own books make one of two mistakes. They either:

1) Throw their dart randomly all over the wall and accomplish little or nothing, or ...

2) Aim their dart at the proper boards, but the message is so diluted, the dart doesn't stick to any of them

The solution: Create a Brand Identity Statement (BIS) about your book and topic. A BIS is a simple but powerful sentence of no more than 15 words (10 words or less is even better) that describes the specific vision and benefit your book delivers.

If you could take every feature and positive aspect associated with your book and subject matter, and run them through a grinder, only to be left with the pure, concentrated essence of what your book is about ... that would be your Brand Identity Statement.

You should craft your BIS to include a benefit statement to your fans. Two well-known BIS's from the traditional business world are Domino's "Fresh, hot pizza delivered to your door in 30 minutes or less, guaranteed" (13 words) and M&M's "Melts in your mouth, not in your hands" (eight words).

Brand Identity Statements in Action

The BIS I use to promote my TheBuzzFactor.com web site is "Music marketing tips and self-promotion ideas for independent songwriters, musicians and bands." For my book Branding Yourself Online, the subtitle serves as the BIS: "How to Use the Internet to Become a Celebrity or Expert in Your Field."

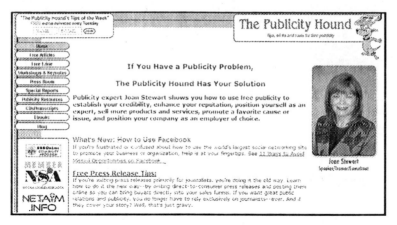

"The Publicity Hound" is Joan Stewart's Brand Identity Statement

Here are some good examples of Brand Identity Statements used by successful authors:

- Alexandria Brown is "The Ezine Queen."

- Joan Stewart goes by "The Publicity Hound."

- Gary Ryan Blair is known as "The Goals Guy."

Can you guess what each of them does? Do you know what their books are about? And all from three words each!

Want more examples? Go to author David Meerman Scott's web site and you'll find the BIS "Online thought leadership and viral marketing strategies using news releases, blogs, podcasts, and online media." It's almost too long at 15 words, but it still does the trick.

Important: Ideally, the title of your book will act as a Brand Identity Statement too, as in:

- *The UltraSimple Diet: Kick-Start Your Metabolism and Safely Lose Up to 10 Pounds in 7 Days*

- *Getting Things Done: The Art of Stress-Free Productivity*

- *The 7 Habits of Highly Effective People*

Is there any doubt as to what these books deliver? Do you know instantly whether or not these topics are for you?

That's why you need a Brand Identity Statement. It greatly increases the odds that your promotional dart will reach and stick to the right types of readers and fans.

7

Build Your #1 Marketing Asset

I've been a published author since 1992, when a small publisher put out my first book, called *101 Ways to Make Money in the Music Business*. I've been promoting myself online since 1995. Guess what I've found to be my strongest book promotion and sales tool?

My web site? Amazon.com? Media exposure?

Nope.

My #1 book marketing asset is my mailing list. That's right, it's the thousands of people over the years who willingly gave me their name and email address and, in essence, have said, "Hey, I'm interested in what you write about. I'd like more information, so keep me posted."

Before I'd ever heard the term "ezine," I realized the power of email. In fact, I didn't even have a proper web site until 1999. So for the first four years I was online, I used other people's web sites and my own mailing list to spread my ideas. And it worked!

Key point: If you want to promote yourself effectively online, you need to start building a mailing list of people interested in you and your ideas. And start doing it yesterday!

Without a growing list, you become a passive book

promoter who sits on the sidelines and hopes that people respond to the messages you put out. With a mailing list, you become a proactive marketer who controls the flow of information directly to the people who need it the most: your potential buyers and fans.

Publishing an email newsletter is not the exhausting chore that some make it out to be. In fact, here are four services that can help you manage your email database and delivery. The first two are free; the last two are fee-based:

Yahoo Groups
http://groups.yahoo.com/

Google Groups
http://groups.google.com/

Constant Contact
www.constantcontact.com

AWeber
www.aweber.com

Bottom line: Start building a mailing list now! Enough said.

#8
Inspire People to Subscribe with an Ethical Bribe

When I started building my mailing list many years ago, email was a fun new tool. It was a lot easier to get people to sign up and for the messages I sent to actually get delivered and read.

Granted, it's a different world today. People are overwhelmed with overflowing Inboxes. And what subscribers don't delete, the spam filters may send to Never Never Land.

You know the drill. But you still need a mailing list. Don't write it off. People still open and read messages from trusted sources who deliver information that's relevant to their lives.

Essential: It's just that these days people need an extra incentive to get more email sent to them. In general, placing a simple "get on my mailing list" sign-up form on your web site won't generate a huge response. And that's where the "ethical bribe" can be a big help.

It's not really a bribe so much as an incentive you dangle in front of the reader and prospective buyer. In essence, you offer something for free from your web site — the first three chapters of your book, an audio interview, a step-by-step checklist, or special report.

Make it something of value, and be sure the subject matter of the freebie will attract your ideal

Subscribe to my free ezine and I'll send you my top secret 'Self-Publishing Confidential' report ... FREE!

In this "insider's guide to self-publishing success," I reveal my best advice, including:

- 4 Ways to Attract More Readers (and Buyers) Faster

- *The 4 Debilitating Myths That Hold Back Most Self-Publishers*

- The Best Way to Promote Your Book Right Now

CONFIDENTIAL

The "ethical bribe" I use on my FullTimeAuthor.com site.

customer and fan. Also, for your convenience and theirs, make the giveaway item something that can be downloaded immediately after their free online subscription has been completed.

Examples: On my FullTimeAuthor.com site, I give away a free copy of my "Self-Publishing Confidential" report. On my TheBuzzFactor.com music site, subscribers get my "Indie Music Marketing Secrets" report.

How do you deliver the immediate download? Most email management systems allow you to create an automated welcome message that gets sent to every new subscriber. Just include the download link in that welcome message and you're set.

If you're not currently offering an incentive to motivate more mailing list subscribers, get cracking and create one now!

#9
Communicate with Your Readers Regularly

Okay, so you've got a mailing list up and running, and new people are signing up all the time. Congratulations! But you're only halfway done. The second part of the mailing list equation is using it. Yes, you have to communicate with these people!

Ideally, you should send something to your list on a regular schedule: once a week, every other week, once a month. I recommend you send something at least monthly — and more often if you can.

Author Marcia Yudkin delivers a weekly "Marketing Minute" email. Mary Lou Andre emails a wardrobe "Tip of the Month." Joe Vitale sends out email messages just about every day (which is probably a bit much for most authors and readers). So find a frequency that works for you, and don't go long stretches where subscribers don't hear from you at all.

Key: Also, don't let the terms "email newsletter" or "ezine" intimidate you. Email messages to your list don't have to be long. In fact, it's much better if they're short and to the point. People will be more likely to open your emails if they know it won't take a lot of their time. Your messages will also be more warmly received if you deliver some nugget of value along with any sales pitch.

Don't have anything new to say? Sure you do.

Point your subscribers to a new article you've posted online. Make them aware of your media appearances and live events. Share a personal experience that inspired you.

More ideas: Hold a contest or offer a discount. Ask for input on the next book you're writing. Make them aware of helpful web sites and resources you've found that they should know about.

In short, think about the needs of your subscribers and ask yourself, "What's the most helpful thing I can deliver to my readers in a timely manner?"

Then deliver it.

#10
Embrace the Best Way to Build Your Book Career

By now you should know that I'm a full-time author. I sustain myself almost exclusively from sales of printed books, ebooks and audio programs — mostly on the subject of music marketing. I run a one-man publishing operation from home.

Unlike many other authors, I rarely supplement my income with speaking or consulting fees. It would probably be smart if I did offer these services more, but I get the most joy from writing and publishing information for my target audience.

Because reaching this full time author/publisher status is rare, both aspiring and veteran authors approach me for advice. Often, they are looking for tips, tricks and shortcuts to success — the best media connection, the most effective marketing angle, or the best way to spend their money so they can reach their publishing goals faster.

Truth: I understand this desire. Everyone wants to get to the destination and enjoy the benefits sooner rather than later. So if you really want to unravel the mystery of publishing success, here it is ...

The biggest secret to share with you is something I call "chipping away at success." There was no one connection, review or sales promotion that put me

over the top. It was an accumulation of little things —
done consistently over weeks, months and years —
that led to the positive word of mouth and recognition
I enjoy today.

So many authors and publishers focus on a big
launch and media blitz with a new title. There's
nothing wrong with that, but I've found the sure and
steady, long-term approach to be most effective for
me.

Your Promotional Canvas

Think of the way an artist paints a picture. First
there's a sketch of what the artist envisions. Then
some broad strokes are put down as the background.
As layers of color are added, a picture begins to
emerge. Each new layer adds detail until a crystal
clear image is formed.

My book promotion history has been a similar
process. I put my focus on two topics I am passionate
about: music and self-promotion. My vision was
similar to the bare sketch an artist creates. Then I
used whatever avenues were available at any given
time to get my message out to the people who
needed to hear it the most: musician readers with a
do-it-yourself mindset.

Action steps: I wrote dozens of articles and
placed them on my own web site and made them
available to countless others. I published an ezine,
contributed to newsgroups and online forums, posted
press releases, gave away promotional ebooks, and
made lots of new friends via email. In more recent
years I've added a blog, a podcast, and video content.

The Snowball Effect

All of these efforts act like layers of paint that build up over time. At first, the image is fuzzy and only a handful of people know who you are and what you do. As you continue to spread your message and leave little promotional crumbs across the Internet, your notoriety slowly expands. Eventually, a multiplying effect takes hold and thousands of people are hearing about you and responding.

Insight: The thing is, no one email, article, sample chapter, or blog post makes a huge splash by itself. It's the combined effect of all your marketing efforts that builds over time. They are drops in a bucket that turn into a steady trickle and, before you know it, a full-blown waterfall that erupts into a tidal wave.

That's my secret to success.

Hopefully, using this same method will allow you to reach your book publishing goals too. Now get busy reading the rest of this book and start leaving your own promotional crumbs somewhere online!

Section Two

Creating a Highly Effective Author Web Site

Register a Memorable Domain Name

As you may know, a domain name is your address on the Internet. It is what people type into a web browser to find you online. Yahoo.com, NPR.org, and EarthLink.net are all examples of domain names. As a self-promoting author or book publisher, you need one too.

Domain names are pretty easy to get. You simply use a domain name registrar, which is a company authorized to assign domain names. The whole transaction can take place online. Here are three domain name registrar sites (with rates ranging from roughly $9 to $15 a year):

GoDaddy
www.godaddy.com

DirectNic
www.directnic.com

Buy Domains
www.buydomains.com

When you're on one of these sites, you can search for available domain names. Just type in a name you want and hit the submit button. The service will let you know right away if the name is available as a .com, .net, .org, and more.

Tip: I recommend you find a name that is available as a .com address. It's too hard to train people to type .net and the others.

The best place to start searching is with your actual name. If you are John Smith, then JohnSmith.com would be ideal. Another great option is the title of your book. If you published *The Secret Guide to Turtlenecks*, then SecretGuideToTurtlenecks.com would be perfect.

If you have a common name, or if your book title uses a common phrase, it may already be taken. If that's the case, see if you can add another word, especially if it's related to your topic, such as:

JohnSmithMysteries.com

JohnSmithGardeningTips.com

SmithGraphicNovels.com

SecretTurtleneckBook.com

TurtleneckSecrets.com

Key: The trick is to choose a domain name that is memorable, easy to spell, and relates directly to what your book is about.

For instance, BlagojevichChiropracticBooks.com is a weak domain name. There are too many ways to misspell it. But BoneBooksOnline.com has a fighting chance of being remembered and typed into a web browser correctly.

You may think all of the good .com domain names are taken. But you might be surprised by how many good ones are still left.

If you haven't already done so, go claim yours today!

#12
Create a Purpose-Driven Web Site

Once you've got your domain name squared away, there's one more thing you should do before you start designing your site: get clear about the purpose of your author web site.

Yes, in general, you are putting up a web site to create awareness online and to have an Internet presence. But the purpose of your web site extends beyond those basics.

To help you define your site's purpose, ask yourself this key question:

What do I want people to *do* when they visit my web site?

Here are some possible answers:

- find out when and where my live events are

- discover where my books are available for sale

- purchase my books directly from my site

- sign up for my email list

- understand the type of material I cover and how it benefits them

- listen to samples of my spoken-word audio

- see what I look like

- watch a video of me

- hire me as a speaker or consultant

Also ask this question:

What do I want people to *think* and *feel* when they visit my web site?

In other words, what emotional response do you want to elicit from your visitors?

Possible answers include:

- empowered and inspired
- sad and melancholy
- turned on and aroused
- outraged and angry
- silly and fun-loving
- relaxed and mellow
- energized and ready to take action

Warning: Please don't say you want your web site to accomplish "all of the above." That's asking too much. Prioritize the actions, thoughts and feelings you want your site to evoke.

Most authors and book publishers never consider these important details — to their detriment. You must clarify your web site *do*, *think* and *feel* goals first. Only then can you design a site that will gently lead people to take the actions and think the thoughts that are most important to you.

13

Take Control of Your Author Web Site Design

When it comes to designing and updating your web site, you basically have three choices:

- **Do it all yourself**. If you have the skills and design sense, you will save a lot of money by creating and updating your web site yourself. Of course, it will take many hours of your time to go this route. But you will have the satisfaction of building your site your way.

- **Delegate all the work to someone else**. With this option, you save time and avoid many potential headaches ... but you must either spend money to hire a designer, or find someone who is competent and willing to help you for little or no money on an ongoing basis.

- **Have someone design your site template; you do updates yourself**. This is the sweet middle ground. Hire a professional to create the overall look and navigation for your web site. But you learn enough skills to make changes yourself.

Where do you stand on these three options?

If you truly want to be an effective online book promoter, I suggest you give this some serious thought.

If you choose the first or third option on the previous page, you'll need some type of web design software. Common applications include FrontPage (microsoft.com/frontpage) and Dreamweaver (adobe.com/products/dreamweaver).

Tip: A good low-cost web design software maker with free versions of its applications is CoffeeCup at www.coffeecup.com/freestuff.

Also, the site design application iWeb comes installed on all new iMacs.

If you don't have the interest or time to design your site yourself, that's fine. You'll be better off having someone with experience create it anyway. However, keep in mind that once the site is up and running, it will need to be updated. How will that be handled? How long will you have to wait for your designer to get to it, and how much will that cost you?

Best advice: If you hire someone to create your site for you, learn enough basic HTML to make changes yourself. Yes, it may take time now to get familiar with it, but you'll be happier in the long run.

To start your web design education, here are two sites that offer solid advice:

How to Build Web Sites
www.how-to-build-websites.com

Web Site Tips
www.websitetips.com

Another design option is to host your site at a paid, template-driven service like AmericanAuthor.com or GoDaddy.com's WebSite Tonight. Services like these are made for non-techie types who want to manage their own web sites. The main drawback is that they can look generic, since many people use the same templates.

What if you're totally broke, don't want to hire a designer, and don't know anyone who can help you? Well, these may not be the ideal long-term solutions, but here are some places where you can build and host a web site for free:

Google Sites
sites.google.com

Terapad
www.terapad.com

Webnode
www.webnode.com

Weebly
www.weebly.com

Wix
www.wix.com

Additional tip: Yet another option is use a free blogging platform like WordPress (at wordpress.org) to create your entire site.

As you can see, there are many ways to take control of your web site design. So if you haven't done so already, pick one and go for it. You can always evolve and upgrade later. The main thing is to get busy pursuing one of these options now!

#14
Make Your Home Page Clear and Easy to Understand

Your web site's home page is the welcome mat of your online presence. Don't confuse people and scare them away before they even take their first step inside your personal domain.

Tip: This should be obvious, but just in case it isn't, please don't assault people with a dizzying array of bells, whistles, and other nonsense when they visit your home on the Internet.

Don't use Flash intro pages, no matter how much your designer says they're cool. (Flash is a popular multimedia platform that adds animation and interactivity to web pages. It has it's place, but can be overused.) And don't make your site too graphics heavy. An author web site can look attractive without overwhelming a visitor's eyes and their web browser's ability to render pages.

Great. You know what *not* to do. Now here are some things you *should do* to make your home page appealing and effective:

- **Fit the most important info into one screen**. The idea here is to avoid long, scrolling pages. That means being ruthlessly terse and pithy with the amount of "stuff" you place on your home page. On interior pages you can get away with more text and content, but resist the urge to tell

Note how I use these elements on my TheBuzzFactor.com web site: white space, eye anchors, calls to action, and more.

---

your entire story right up front. Too much information too soon may actually chase some people away — and that won't help you sell more books.

- **Use plenty of "white space."** Along with being selective about the amount of information you initially throw at people, also be kind to your web visitors' eyes. Don't cram too many things too close together. Give your web pages space to breathe. Your readers will thank you and stay longer on your web site if you do.

- **Make it more than a sales pitch**. One of the common web design mistakes I see authors and publisher make is turning their home page into a giant "Buy Now" button. Sure, you want to let people know you have books for sale. But that's not the sole purpose of having a web site. In addition, your site should be set up to highlight samples of your work, inspire people to subscribe to your email updates, and more.

- **Focus on the upper left**. Research has shown that web users look first at the upper left corner of a web page, then work their way down and to the right. So place your name, book cover, or an eye-catching image in this powerful, upper left-hand corner. (Scott Turow's home page at www.scottturow.com is a good example of this.)

- **Give visitors "eye anchors."** People generally scan most web sites. So don't place lots of long, scrolling text on your pages. Instead, use short paragraphs, bullet points, book cover images, and bold sub headlines to draw attention to the things you want people to read, know about, and click on.

- **Spell out your "call to action."** On each page of your author web site, you should have a goal — something you want a visitor to DO while on that page. It might be read an excerpt, subscribe to your ezine, come to an event, purchase a book, etc. Whatever it is, make that clear and include a call to action — clear instructions to do that thing now.

- **Watch someone surf your web site**. Corporate types call this usability research. You can call it whatever you want, but you'll learn a lot by simply watching different people go to your web site for the first time, even if they are just friends and family members. Don't interrupt or make suggestions. Just observe. Then ask and answer questions. This exercise will prove invaluable when it comes to making your web site better.

Another thing you can do is visit lots of other authors' web sites and simply note what you like and dislike about them. Try to incorporate your favorite features and keep a watchful eye on the negative design aspects that may have accidently slipped into your own web site. Then correct them as soon as possible.

15

Be Crystal Clear About What You and Your Book Offer

Here's the main point I want to make with this section: Always view your web site (and all of your online marketing efforts, for that matter) through the eyes of someone discovering you for the first time.

Don't ever assume that a person visiting your web site already knows who you are, what you write about, and why that's such a great thing. Try to imagine what someone stumbling upon your site will think as they set their eyes upon it for the first time.

Ask yourself these questions:

- Is the web page clear and easy to understand?

- Do you make it obvious what your book's subject matter and genre are?

- Do you give people a reason to click deeper into your web site to learn more?

- If someone arrives at your site on a page other than the home page, will they still know immediately what it's all about?

It seems so obvious, but you'd be surprised by the vast number of vague and mysterious author web sites scattered about the Internet. They feature a large photo of the author, his or her name, and cryptic verbiage such as, "A great read" or "Winner of four book awards" or, my favorite, "Once you start reading, you won't be able to put this book down!"

Sadly, few people will ever pick up this author's book, because the web site doesn't provide a clue as to what it is and how it benefits the reader.

Suggestion: At the top of every page on your web site, include a short and lively, benefit-oriented reference to the type of material you write.

Examples:

- Author Katherine Woodward Thomas uses "7 Weeks to Attract the Love of Your Life" on her web site.

- Brenda Novak's home page starts with "NY Times Bestselling Romantic Suspense Author."

- Corinne Richardson uses the phrase "Helping people simplify the second half of their lives."

- On my music promotion site, you'll find "Music marketing tips and self-promotion ideas for independent songwriters, musicians and bands" at the top of every page.

Is there any doubt what these sites, authors and books offer? No.

Do you know right away if each site is (or is not) for you? Of course you do!

Now make sure your web site is equally clear and specific.

#16
Push Benefits on Your Web Site, Not Your Book

This is one of the most difficult concepts for most authors (and self-promoters in general) to grasp. But here is the honest truth:

The best way to promote and sell your book online is to NOT promote your book ... directly.

What the heck do I mean? Let me explain ...

I understand why there's so much confusion over this. The thought process often starts with the idea "I need to take action to sell my book." And the common term that describes this activity is *self*-promotion. Therefore, when an author or publisher takes action to promote, the focus is usually on the author and the book.

Go to most book web sites and you'll see the author's photo, an image of the book cover, and a list of facts: where the book is available for sale, how many awards it has won, where the author is from, what educational degrees he has earned, where the author is speaking, etc.

All that stuff is fine. But it's not the primary thing that the visitors to your web site care about. So, what do they care about?

What's in it for them!

That means your job is to make certain the most

prominent words that appear on your web site focus on the benefits to your readers and fans.

Question: What really motivates someone to purchase your book? It's not just your credentials or experience or magnificent writing style. The reason they part with their money is because of the way they believe your book will enhance their life.

Time and time again I've explained this essential concept to new authors. And, sure enough, when I later saw their web sites, they were filled with "My book has won this, I've done that, I, me, mine ... blah, blah, blah!"

Reality: Human beings naturally gravitate toward talking and thinking about themselves. And for good reason. For millions of years, members of our species had to focus on their own needs to survive. In the caveman days, if you weren't consumed with self-preservation, you'd be consumed by any number of wild predators, not to mention being done in by members of rival tribes. There's a long-standing tradition of human self-indulgence.

Instead of getting depressed by this news, you can use it to your advantage — first, by resisting this primitive egocentric urge when it comes to promoting your book, and second, by being aware of the lens through which all potential buyers are viewing your web site.

So, when someone visits your site for the first time, who will they focus on? Don't kid yourself and think it's you.

Do this: Give readers what they want and make sure your marketing message hits them squarely on the head with what's in it for them. Lead off with the number one benefit fans get from you, followed by the number two benefit, and so on. Pile the motivating reasons they should care about your book one on top of the other until even the most thick-headed of humans can figure it out.

A strange example: Let's say you were put in charge of marketing a new electric drill for home-owners. How would you go about it?

Most people would start listing features: the manufacturer, mechanical specs, and material the drill is made of ... all focusing on — you guessed it — the drill.

But what do people really want when they buy a drill?

A hole.

They also want a hole that can be created quickly, easily and economically. It really doesn't matter if the hole gets there because of a drill, a toaster, a pair of socks, or a monk — as long as the appropriate hole is conveniently creating in the appropriate place.

In other words, *sell the hole*, not the drill. Then, and only then, use your features to show how your drill can meet the customer's specific needs.

#17

Make the Best Use of
Features and Feelings

The previous section addressed the classic marketing principle of separating features from benefits. You've probably heard it before. But sadly, no matter how often people hear it, they rarely put it into action. So this topic deserves a little more attention before we move on.

To demonstrate how to transform features into benefits, I'll use the way I've marketed my spoken-word audio books. I'll list each feature first, then its corresponding benefit.

Feature: Sixty minutes in length.

Benefit: Jam-packed with a full hour of career-boosting details you can start using the same day you order.

Feature: Available only in audio format.

Benefit: Soak up these useful success secrets at your convenience: while you drive, jog, ride a bike, or clean the house. Audio books make learning easy.

Feature: It's an MP3 download.

Benefit: Why wait? Start putting these ideas to use immediately. Get instant access as soon as your order is approved online.

Get the idea? You must learn to do the same thing when describing your books.

One Final Important Point

Yes, factual details about you and your book will help persuade some people to buy. But most will become fans for a reason that has nothing to do with facts and features. They will be attracted to you because of the way your book, personality, and perspective make them feel.

That's right ... *feel*.

The most powerful response you can get from someone is based on emotion and the way your writing style and book affects them physically and mentally, and sometimes spiritually. Author and speaker Tony Robbins refers to this mysterious phenomenon as a "state change."

Key: Your most hardcore fans will react to your writings in a way that makes them feel different (and usually much better) while they absorb your ideas. Their heart rate and body chemistry will actually shift as they read your words.

And sometimes, after they know you, the shift may occur when they merely see your picture, hear you speak, or read about you (like a book lover's version of Pavlov's dog).

It's your job as a self-promoter to understand the powerful effect your writing style and ideas have, and to use that knowledge to spread those great feelings to even more people.

For example, you could announce:

"Self-published author from Kansas City publishes new book about growing better flowers."

Or ... you could say something more "state change"-oriented like:

"There's nothing quite like the feeling of sinking your hands into the earth and adding beauty to the exterior of your home. And when the neighbors compliment you, the glow of personal pride will swell within you."

See the difference?

From now on, always use this principle to attract more readers, buyers and fans!

18

Make Sure Your Navigation Is Simple and Obvious

As you should know by now, the design of your home page is crucial. It's the entrance to your online domain, and it offers a strong first impression and easy access to vital information.

But your home page is simply the doorway that leads visitors to other "rooms" within your online home. You must now decide what rooms to build, and then create clearly marked interior doors that lead to them.

Important: The term "navigation" is used to describe the way you lead people around your web site. Every page of your site should include a consistent set of links or tabs that list the sections where you want visitors to go. These links should appear in the same location on every page.

(Note how I've structured the navigation for my music site at TheBuzzFactor.com. Click any of the tabs near the top and you'll see that they appear in the same place throughout the site.)

Every author web site is different, but what follows are 11 of the most common navigation link categories. But *don't use all of them*. Choose the five or six links that make the most sense for your site:

- **Home.** Your navigation should always include an easy way for people to get to your welcome mat:

your home page. That should ideally be a link that actual says "Home." However, some sites use a clickable site name logo in the top left corner of every page that takes people back home. This has become fairly common, but you can't go wrong with the more direct "Home" link.

- **Bio**. Sometimes called "About," this section is where people go to read your bio. Use this page to go into some depth about your background and experiences. Don't clutter up your home page with your life history. Just give visitors a taste of who you are, then send them here to learn more.

- **Books**. This is the link you want people to click to find out more about your books and other products. On this page you can give visitors sample chapters, display glowing testimonials and, of course, let them know how they can purchase each title. This section can also be labeled "Store" or "Buy."

- **Events**. Send people here to learn more about your upcoming speaking events and live work-shops. Be sure to list all pertinent information about dates, venues, times, and locations. Other words commonly used for this link include "Live" and "Calendar."

- **Press**. Also called "Media" or "News," this section often features a list of where you've been covered in the press, along with review excerpts and links to online articles. It can also include an online "media room" where journalists can find photos, press releases, and other items that address their needs.

- **Blog**. If you publish a web log of your ideas and experiences (especially if you add new posts regularly), you can add a blog link to your navigation choices.

- **Video**. Some authors make good use of online video. If that describes you, set aside a place on your web site where fans can view your video clips.

- **Hire**. If you make yourself available for coaching or consulting work related to your book, be sure to include a link where people can learn more about your services. Other words that can be used for the navigation to this page include "Consulting," "Coaching" and "Services."

- **Forum**. If you encourage your fans to interact with each other, adding a discussion forum on your site may be a good idea — but only if a good number of fans really use it. If it sits dormant most of the time, don't bother.

- **Subscribe**. In addition to having an email list sign-up form on your home page, you can also place this form in the same location on every page, along with your navigation links. Another option is to display a "Subscribe" link or tab that takes visitors to a page that spells out the benefits of getting on your list, assures them that you won't abuse their email address, etc.

- **Contact**. Every set of web site navigation links should include a "Contact" option. On this page, include your physical address, phone numbers, and email contacts for booking, publicity, fan messages, etc.

Web design tip: Try to keep the name of each navigation link to one word, if at all possible. Note how I used only one word in all of the previous examples. It makes it easier to design and use.

Here's another thing to consider when designing your navigation links — and your entire web site, for that matter. We covered it in the previous "Create a Purpose-Driven Web Site" section. Think long and hard about what you want people to *do, think and feel* when they come to your author web site.

What are your top priorities?

Action step: As you design your pages (or instruct someone else to), make sure the layout and navigation choices emphasize your top goals and lead visitors to the actions you desire.

Another important key to effective web site navigation is this ...

Limit your visitors' choices!

Don't bombard people with too much information or too many options. As I've stressed before, people don't need to know everything about you right off the bat. Limit their choices to the five or six areas that are most important to you, your readers, and your book publishing goals.

#19
Become a Resource, Not Just a Book Seller

In his popular business relationship book, *Never Eat Alone*, Keith Ferrazzi writes, "People do business with people they know, like and trust."

That's a simple but potent sentence.

Some book buyers will make a purchase the first time they visit your site. Hopefully, a lot of them will. But for most of your web site visitors, it will take time. It will require repeated exposures to your message before they feel they truly know, like and trust you.

Insight: One of the best ways to move that process along is to not think of yourself as an author, a publisher, or a book seller. But to instead consider yourself a resource on your genre, topic or area of expertise.

John Kremer is a great example of this. Sure, he sells books and resources on book marketing from his web site at www.Bookmarket.com. But his site is also packed with dozens of resource pages filled with marketing tips, book publishing statistics, directories, and more. Kremer has been compiling and freely sharing much of this information for years.

By making sure it is far more than a simple sales site for his books, Kremer's site has become a must-see destination for aspiring authors and book

John Kremer does a good job of positioning Bookmarket.com as a resource destination; not simply a place where he sells books.

---

promoters. Building that type of reputation is priceless.

The same can be said for my TheBuzzFactor.com site, where I offer a virtual warehouse of free music marketing tips and ideas. There you'll find years of content delivered via a free ezine, blog, podcast, articles, video clips, and more.

I estimate that more than 70% of everything I've ever written about music marketing has been freely shared on the Internet in bite-sized chuncks through various means. And, as a result, my reputation has grown and my book sales increase every year.

Key question: What information can you provide on your web site to make it a valuable resource for your ideal readers and fans?

#20
Become the Premier Giver in Your Genre

Are you a giver or a hoarder? A giver is eager to share a lot of her knowledge and expertise with anyone who's interested. A hoarder wants to keep all of his finely crafted words and ideas under lock and key.

I've seen both types of authors. Interestingly enough, givers end up getting more than hoarders ever do.

Hoarders are paranoid that people are out to steal their stuff. They worry about copyright protection and their intellectual property. That's fine, but I can tell you that few authors are ever victims of copyright infringement. But most are victims of another curse: *obscurity*.

Insight: Most successful authors realize they have a lot to share. So they regularly write and distribute free articles and reports. They do interviews and public speaking events. They even give away sample chapters (and sometimes the entire text) of their books — all in an effort to become known to their target audience. These smart authors know, once they create awareness with the right people, their careers and book sales will take off.

Janet Switzer is a giver. She is the author of *Instant Income* and co-author of *The Success*

Principles with Jack Canfield. Her approach is different from John Kremer and others who create resource destination web sites.

Take a look at Switzer's web sites (www.HowExpertsBuildEmpires.com and www.InstantIncome.com) and you'll notice they are primarily "squeeze pages" designed to capture names and email addresses for her mailing list. But once she gets you on her list, she delivers a lot: special reports, articles, and checklists to help you turn your ideas into revenue.

Question: Why does she give this stuff away? Because she has higher priced products and services that she references within these free items. All it takes is a small percentage of the people on her list to buy and she'll make a nice profit.

And what about all the rest who don't purchase something from Switzer? Well, many will think of her as someone who delivered great value and may recommend her to someone else who will hire her. They will expand her positive word-of-mouth reputation, and her career will continue to grow.

See. It pays to be a giver.

So start sharing and giving ... and reaping the benefits!

#21

Make Smart Use of Your Web Page Title Tags

There's a lot of hype about search engine rankings and how to trick Google and Yahoo into listing your web site high for your chosen keywords. Let's ignore most of that noise and concentrate on one simple thing you can do to help the way your site gets listed in search results.

I'm talking about Title tags.

Title tags are included in the HTML source code of your pages. The words you use between `<title>` and `</title>` determine what appears in the top title bar of your web browser. Search engines use these tags as one way to determine the content of web pages.

So, be sure to load your title tags with the words that potential customers might use to search for books and information like yours. Here are some examples ...

Poor use of Title tags:

```
<title>Snuggle Doodle Home Page</title>
```

This is a common way that authors waste an opportunity to connect with readers online. Simply putting the name of the author or the book in Title tags is fine, especially if you know that people are searching specifically for your name or your book's title. But that's just the start.

Ideally, you want people to find you online when they are searching for your topic, genre, or area of expertise — not just your name or book title. Therefore, your Title tags should include words and phrases that people who need what you publish will enter into Google.

Now let's consider a rewrite of the previous example ...

Good use of Title tags:

```
<title>Snuggle Doodle - Books and music
for children, toddlers and kids of all
ages</title>
```

This tag is much more effective. It is based on the educated assumption that potential buyers are searching online using phrases such as "children's books with music," "music for kids," and "music books for children." Notice how all of those words appear in the Title tag above. (Note: Please don't search for Snuggle Doodle; I made it up.)

Tip: Each page on your site should have a different Title tag based on the content of that page. For instance, if the author of the Snuggle Doodle series also had a page of free music downloads, the Title tag for that page might read:

```
<title>Free music for kids, children's
music downloads</title>
```

See how this works? It's all about being as clear, specific and descriptive as possible.

22

Make Sure Your Web Pages Are Search Engine Friendly

To improve your chances of ranking well in search engine results, the words that appear throughout a web page should compliment the words that appear in that page's Title, Meta Description and Meta Keywords tags.

These two online tools will help you analyze your pages for free:

Keyword Density Analyser

tools.seobook.com/general/keyword-density/

Meta Tag Analyzer

www.submitexpress.com/analyzer/

Not sure what all this talk about meta tags and keyword density is about? It's a topic beyond the scope of this book, but it is important stuff to know. So check out these three online resources for further guidance:

META Tag Guide

www.submitcorner.com/Guide/Meta/

Meta tags - what, where, when, why?

www.philb.com/metatag.htm

Keyword Density

www.seochat.com/seo-tools/keyword-density/

#23
Add Interactivity to Your Author Web Site

One way to get people involved with you and your book is to give them something to do while they're on your web site. That's why you should add some kind of interactive element, such as a poll, audio player, guest book, message forum, ecards, etc.

There's a good reason you should do this. Think about what happens when you stop by a car lot to shop for a new auto. The salesperson always asks if you want to take one of the vehicles you're eyeing for a test drive. Why?

Insight: Getting behind the wheel gets you physically involved with the car. Your senses are stimulated and you directly experience what it would be like to own it. If you enjoy the experience, you'll begin to visualize the car being yours and will mentally start taking ownership of the vehicle.

That interaction makes you much more likely to purchase the car than if you simply looked at it from a distance or just viewed a photo of it.

How does this relate to books? Think about it. Have you ever purchased a book after picking it up and thumbing through it at a bookstore?

Visiting a web site is often similar to viewing a picture of a car. It's a distant relationship with it. You're goal is to engage your online visitors. Give them something to do. Motivate them to click, or express themselves in some way, or subscribe, or read a sample chapter.

Here are some sites that provide interactive tools for free:

Bravenet
www.bravenet.com

Mister Poll
www.misterpoll.com

Widgetbox
www.widgetbox.com

Sparklit
www.sparklit.com

Survey Monkey
www.surveymonkey.com

Tip: Also check out AdaptiveBlue's free book widgets at www.getglue.com/book-widgets. Many prominent authors are using these, so there there may be something to them.

The main takeaway from this section is that anything you can do to involve your web visitors in your book and its topic is a good thing.

#24
Accept Payments from Your Web Site

The title of this guide is *55 Ways to Promote & Sell Your Book on the Internet*. We've covered a lot of the "promote" part — and there's more coming. Now let's start dealing with the "sell" aspect. The next few sections will show you the mechanics of selling books directly from your own web site.

Just so you know, it is possible to spend the bulk of your time marketing and still sell a ton of books ... without ever actually selling them from your own site. Some authors simply send people to Amazon, Lulu.com, BookLocker.com, or some other book sales site to make the final purchase. These authors choose not to mess with processing orders and answering customer service emails.

That's fine, and I'll address some of those options in upcoming sections. But many authors (including yours truly) enjoy the greater profits that come from selling directly to customers.

Reality: When you send your fans to Amazon, you may save some time, but you also give up a good chunk of the profit.

In the old days, to accept credit card payments of any kind, you had to get what's called a "merchant account" from a bank. You still can, but there is paperwork involved, monthly service fees, and a lot of hoops to jump through if your business is mostly Internet-based.

These days, especially if you're just getting your feet wet with book sales, there are much easier ways to accept credit card payments online.

Payment Processing Options

Hands down, the easiest way to start accepting orders from your own site is to open a **PayPal Premier/Business account**. It's free and pretty easy to use. There are millions of PayPal users. Plus, PayPal has low fees and flexible access to your money. The site takes between 1.9% and 2.9% of the purchase amount (depending on your monthly sales volume), plus a 30 cent per-transaction fee.

So at the highest fee rate, on a $25 sale, PayPal would take $1.03. That's a small price to pay to be able to accept payments on your web site. Visit www.paypal.com for more information.

Once you are signed up with PayPal, log into your account and click the Merchant Services tab. Then follow the instrcutions to create a "Buy Now" button for your book. Place the code it gives you into your book's sales page and you are ready to start taking orders online. PayPal will alert you by email every time a sale is made.

Myth buster: Years ago, buyers were required to open a free PayPal account to make purchases. But that is no longer the case. Buyers can simply use their credit card like any other online processor. Still, some people prefer not to use PayPal, so it's not a bad idea to give buyers an alternate payment option.

Another service that is primed to be a major competitor to PayPal is **Google Checkout** at checkout.google.com. A relative newcomer to the online shopping arena, it has many of the same functions as PayPal and charges even lower fees (2% of the purchase amount and only 20 cents per transaction). Plus, it's owned by Google, the Internet's premier brand name. That makes Google Checkout another solid online payment option.

Breaking news: As I was going to press with this book, I discovered that Amazon.com had launched a service called Simple Pay with very attractive rates. Learn more at payments.amazon.com.

Beyond that, here are five additional online credit card processing services to consider:

2CheckOut.com
www.2checkout.com

ClickBank (digital products only)
www.clickbank.com

CCnow.com
www.ccnow.com

Authorize.net
www.authorize.net

Merchant Express
www.merchantexpress.com

Look over fees and policies carefully. Most have a per-transaction fee plus a percentage of each sale. Some have an additional monthly service fee. So look them all over and see what works best for you.

#25
Set Up an Effective Shopping Cart System

The previous section showed you an easy way to set up a PayPal "Buy Now" button for a single product. That's a good start. But what if you have multiple titles for sale or sell your book in different formats (paperback, ebook, audio)?

What you need is an online shopping "cart" that will allow your customers to add and subtract titles before they "check out" and make their final purchase. If you've ever bought anything online, you already know how this process works.

When it comes to online shopping carts, you have many options to choose from. In a moment I'll tell you about the system that I and many of the top Internet marketers use. But that may be a little pricey if you're just starting out. Luckily, there are several no-cost and low-cost cart options available.

Tip: The first to consider is, once again, PayPal. In the Merchant Services section of your account you'll also find an "Add to Cart" button option. So, if you're keeping things simple and just sticking with PayPal, use its no-frills shopping cart features.

Likewise, Google Checkout has easy-to-use "Add to Cart" button abilities. Even though I've never used Google for payments, it looks like it has a very clean and efficient cart system.

Bob Baker

Thanks for turning to **Bob Baker** for creative self-promotion ideas and inspiration! Make your purchase using PayPal or most major credit cards. If you prefer not to use PayPal, simply click "Check Out" to proceed to the next screen.

Your Shopping Cart

Quantity	Product	Price	Total	Remove
1	Create a Major Book Buzz Online (MP3 audio, PowerPoint, PDF download)	$14.95	$14.95	x

| | | Subtotal | $14.95 |
| Coupon code (optional) | Apply | **Total:** | **$14.95** |

Continue Shopping | Recalculate | Clear Cart

Check out with **PayPal**
The safer, easier way to pay

Here is the shopping cart page that buyers are taken to when they click the "Add to Cart" button on my web sites.

Hot tip: Another popular option I've been seeing a lot lately (but have not used myself) is a service called **E-Junkie** at www.e-junkie.com. It has an amazing list of features, and you can start using it for only $5 a month.

Note that E-Junkie does not "process" the payments itself. It simply handles the "shopping cart" aspect of each sale. However, it integrates easily with PayPal, Google Checkout, 2CheckOut, ClickBank, and Authorize.net.

The truth: If I was just getting started with selling books online, I would give E-Junkie serious consideration.

There are many other shopping cart systems with prices and technical requirements all over the map. But the Cadillac of Internet shopping carts for years has been a service called **1ShoppingCart**.

In addition to the usual cart features, you can use it to run an affiliate program, send email newsletters, test different sales page offers, send buyers a series of automated follow-up emails, offer discount coupon codes, and much more. Fees range from $29 a month for the basic Autoresponder Package to $99 a month for the full-blown Professional Package.

Yes, that's a good chunk of change. But as your sales volume increases, it's a good option to consider. Visit www.1shoppingcart.com to learn more.

#26
Sell Downloadable Ebooks, Reports, Audio, and More

Before we wrap up this section, let's talk about selling downloadable titles. These would be products that customers order from your web site, download to their own computers, and enjoy without anything being physically shipped to them.

Items that fall into this category include:

- **Ebooks**: Digital versions of your books usually in PDF format

- **Special Reports**: Shorter titles that are often available only as PDF downloads

- **Audio**: Spoken-word versions of your books and reports, or recordings of your live events, usually in MP3 format

- **Video**: Recordings of a live workshops, lectures, or tutorials, in a variety of video formats

- **Other**: You might also offer downloadable PowerPoint files, Excel spreadsheets, or software programs

You can deliver these files in two ways: manually or automatically. The more primitive manual method involves you sending a personal email to every customer who orders a downloadable title.

The main problem with this is the delay factor. If you're away from your computer or travelling for a day or two, you might have an impatient and unhappy customer on your hands.

Tip: The best way is to automate the process. Unfortunately, PayPal and Google Checkout don't have easy or reliable solutions for digital download delivery. However, the E-Junkie shopping cart mentioned in the previous section does have this feature (starting at the $18 a month level).

Another option: If you use 2CheckOut.com to process payments, you can designate a "thank you" page for each title. Customers are sent to this page after a successful payment. You can simply place the download instructions and links on those pages.

But one of your best bets may be to use ClickBank.com. For a one-time $49.95 activation charge and modest per-transaction fees, you get a reliable and widely used system for delivering secure digital downloads.

Bonus: ClickBank also has a great built-in affiliate program. Get other people to promote your titles for you in exchange for a commission on any sales they generate. The best part is that ClickBank tracks all the sales and pays your affiliates for you!

Just keep in mind that ClickBank can be used only for digital products. So you'll need to give buyers another option for ordering physical copies of your book from your web site.

Now that we've covered your web site, in the next section we'll reach out and promote your books on other people's web sites.

Section Three

Promoting Your Book Across the Internet

27

Use a "Hub and Spoke" Marketing System

Once you have an effective author web site created and ready for hungry readers, it's time to start building your presence across the Internet. After all, people need to be aware of your web site before they can visit it. That's what this section and the rest of the book are about: creating awareness and driving traffic to your home on the Web — your author site.

But before you run off and start promoting yourself online, I want you to grasp a new concept. It's so important I've devoted a couple of pages to it alone.

What am I talking about?

My friend Scott Ginsberg (a successful author and speaker) and I have been using the term "octopus marketing" in recent years to describe our approach to marketing online. Yes, I know it sounds "fishy," but bare with me. If you grasp this concept, your Internet book promotion efforts will be a lot more profitable.

Do this: Picture an octopus in your mind. There's a head in the center, and then there are multiple tentacles that stretch out in every direction. It's a great analogy for how you need to view your online book promotion activities.

Your author web site should be at the center of all your Internet marketing efforts. It's your home base.

But as a proactive self-promoter, you don't just create a web site and then sit back and wait for things to magically start happening.

What you do now is reach out and leave traces of yourself (and your book) in as many places as possible across the Internet. Every time you reach out, it's another tentacle extending from your author web site.

If you're not crazy about the squid reference, let's try another analogy: a bicycle tire.

Think of your web site as the hub in the middle. The outside rim of the tire represents all the places online where you have a presence. The spokes are the pathways to and from your author site hub.

Important: The spokes (or tentacles, if you prefer) are two-way pipelines. They represent you proactively reaching out to other web sites and online destinations; but they also act as roadways that lure your ideal customers and fans to your hub.

Some marketing people refer to this concept as "push and pull." You are simultaneously pushing your message out and, by so doing, pulling readers and potential buyers closer to you.

It doesn't matter what words you use to describe it — octopus marketing, a hub and spoke system, push and pull. Whatever you call it, you must ingrain this concept in your mind to be an effective Internet book promoter.

Turn to the next page and we'll move on to another important principle.

#28
Plug Into Topic Filters

This will come as no surprise to you, but I'll state the obvious anyway: The Internet is a crowded and noisy place. There are so many people, so many sites to sift through, so many information sources, so many applications and new widgets, so many choices ... it's staggering.

If you feel that way, just think about your potential readers and book buyers. They feel over-whelmed too.

The good news is, people don't have to wade through everything available online to find what they want. These days, there are a growing number of "filters" that help consumers get exactly the information they need quickly.

What's a filter?

The most prominent and obvious example of a filter is the mega search site Google.com. It's often the first place people go to hunt down information they are looking for.

Facts: Google accounts for about 72% of all search engine usage. Yahoo.com is second with 18% and Live.com (formerly MSN Search) is third with 6%. (These figures are from early 2009. As I was going to press, Microsoft's Bing.com search site was making a splash, so these numbers will no doubt change.)

But search sites aren't the only filters people use to seek out and discover new and useful information online. Other filters include:

- Personal recommendations from friends (the most potent filter of all)
- Customer reviews and ratings
- Trusted bloggers and podcasters
- Coverage in traditional and online media
- Bestseller lists
- Topic-specific web sites

This is just a short list of filter examples, but hopefully it will help to cement another important principle into your ever-expanding marketing mind ...

Key insight: When promoting yourself and your book online, you must tap into the filters that your ideal readers are using to find stuff online!

To demonstrate this concept in action, I chose a specific type of book customer at random: baby boomer-aged women. A quick search turned up these six ideal topic filters:

National Association of Baby Boomer Women
www.nabbw.com

Boomer Women Speak
www.boomerwomenspeak.com

The Feisty Side of Fifty
www.feistysideoffifty.com

Boomer Babes Rock
www.boomerbabesrock.com

Boomer Girl

www.boomergirl.com

Squidoo: Baby Boomer Women

www.squidoo.com/babyboomerwomen

Beyond sites catering specifically to boomer women, there are thousands of sites geared toward baby boomers in general, including:

Aging Hipsters Blog

www.aginghipsters.com/blog

Baby Boomer Magazine

www.babyboomer-magazine.com

My Prime Time

www.myprimetime.com

Boomers International

www.boomersint.org

And these are filter examples for just one type of book buyer.

Bottom line: It's your new mission to seek out the topic filters that *your* ideal readers and potential buyers are using. Then get busy finding the best ways to have a presence at each destination.

29

Create a Trail of "Link Bait"

Hopefully, pieces of the online book promotion puzzle are starting to come together for you and create a clear picture. You now understand the role of your author web site, comprehend the importance of a hub and spoke system, and realize the value of tapping into topic filters.

There's one more concept I want to cover before we get into the mechanics of spreading your message online. I'm talking about "link bait." It's a pretty simple concept, but I'm constantly surprised by how often it eludes even the smartest authors and online promoters.

As the Internet expands, people have become increasingly mesmerized by Web 2.0 technologies, multimedia, and a growing number of interactive features. That's great, but it has caused people to lose sight of an important principle.

Key insight: When it comes to finding things online, the Internet is still a text-based, word-driven medium. When people go to Google, they type in *words* and *phrases* related to what they're looking for.

Likewise, when they are scanning blogs and information sites, they are attracted to headlines and descriptions that contain words directly related to their interests.

Don't underestimate the power of this reality. So many people pay lip service to this idea and say, "Oh yeah, I get it." But when you examine their book promotion efforts, they miss the target.

Don't make this same mistake!

From now on, when you create your tentacles (or spokes), and when you plug into topic filters online, fill them with "link bait." Load them up, in a natural and sensible way, with the words and phrases of interest to your specific type of reader.

For example, if your ideal potential buyers are corporate executives who ride Harley-Davidson motorcycles, then the things you post across the Internet (articles, blog posts, video cips, etc.) should include obvious references that will resonate with these people.

Let's say you distribute a sample chapter from your book, *The Harley Lifestyle Guide for Corporate Executives*. An author who isn't thinking (not you, of course, but many others fall into this category) might simply use the chapter title, "Ditch the Tie and Hit the Road," when posting the sample chapter online.

Question: Seems harmless enough, but how will "Ditch the Tie and Hit the Road" help you reach corporate executives who ride Harleys?

A better, more targeted, "link bait" approach would be to use the title "Corporate Executives Who Love Harley-Davidson Motorcycles (Free Book Chapter)." This is much more effective because it's loaded with words that will attract the ideal reader. It's far more likely to connect with a potential buyer than "Ditch the Tie and Hit the Road."

Really. Think about it. What person in the target market group for this book will be entering the phrase "ditch the tie" into a search engine? But how many of them might stop and take a second look at something that blatantly has the words "Harley-Davidson motorcycles" in it?

See what I mean?

When it comes to marketing online, you must resist the urge to be cute or mysterious. Above all, don't be vague. Spell out exactly what something is so that when your ideal fan sees it, he or she will immediately exclaim, "Yes, that's for me!"

Make link bait your friend. It will be a powerful book promotion ally.

#30
Go Where Book Lovers Already Are Online

By now you know that you need to get exposure online in the places where the people most likely to be attracted to your topic and identity congregate.

Another great thing you should do is have a presence on the sites where book lovers in general are already hanging out and interacting with each other.

Tip: If your book has the potential to be used by book discussion and reading groups, there are many web sites that cater to this audience. The really cool thing about these sites is that some of them bring together the online and offline worlds. If you can use the Internet to connect with a group of readers who meet face to face to discuss book topics, you are blending the best of both worlds.

By making an impact through these sites, you will create awareness online while also connecting with people in a very real way. Books that are discussed and debated in person are far more likey to be remembered (and purchased) than books that people have simply stumbled upon while surfing online.

So give Internet book discussion and reading group forums some serious consideration. Here are several good ones to investigate:

Reading Group Guides
www.readinggroupguides.com

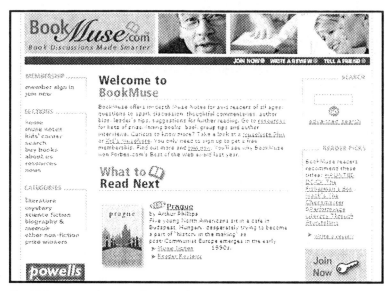

BookMuse.com is one of many sites where readers gather online to discuss their favorite books, genres and topics.

Book Clubs Resource

www.book-clubs-resource.com

Book Muse

www.bookmuse.com

Book Discussion Center

www.bookspot.com/discussion

Book Talk

www.booktalk.org

Biblio Book Discussion

forum.biblio.com

Note: You don't have to be on all of these sites. It would help your sanity and your effectiveness to pick and choose the best sites and work those regularly.

#31
Write and Distribute
Free Articles

There were two things I did early on in my Internet days (back in the mid to late 1990s) that proved to be highly effective at jump-starting my online identity. And I consider both of them to still be rock-solid, fundamental ways to promote books.

One was publishing a free email newsletter, which I covered in Section One. The other thing I did was regularly write articles on my core topic (which, in my case, was music marketing). I took these articles and posted them on my own web site, of course. But I also made them available to any webmaster or ezine publisher who wanted to run them.

I asked for only one thing in return: They simply had to run a blurb, that I supplied, at the end of each article.

Key: In addition to freely giving away my articles to anyone who asked to run them, I also actively sought out web sites, newsletters, magazines, and ezines that could use them.

And, to this day, when I post articles on my own web site, I include a notice on the page that reads:

```
FREE Reprint Rights - You may publish this
article in your ezine or on your web site as
long as you include the following author
bio/blurb at the end of the article:
```

Bob Baker is the author of "55 Ways to Promote & Sell Your Book on the Internet," "Self-Publishing Success Secrets," and "Guerrilla Music Marketing Handbook." He is a full-time author, past president of the St. Louis Publishers Association, and a regular presenter at IBPA's Publishing University. Download a free copy of his "Self-Publishing Confidential" report at FullTimeAuthor.com.

Over the years, this simple technique alone has led to my words appearing on many thousands of web sites across the Internet. And all of them carry a blurb about me and my books, with a link back to my web site.

Truth: In the old days, the main way to get your articles posted was to actively seek out sites that would run them. These days it's a lot easier, mostly because of the growth of "article repository" web sites.

These sites exist for the sole purpose of showcasing a huge warehouse of free articles on every topic imaginable. Webmasters and ezine publishers regularly browse them in search of new content to share with their readers.

Here are the four main sites I recommend for article distribution:

EzineArticles
www.ezinearticles.com

Idea Marketers
www.ideamarketers.com

93

IdeaMarketers.com is one of many sites where you can post and distribute your articles to editors looking for fresh content.

iSnare

www.isnare.com

Article City

www.articlecity.com

Use something similar to the reprint rights notice I highlighted earlier on your own web site and seek out sites that can use your articles, in addition to posting them on one or more of the article sites above.

Doing so will go a long way toward spreading your message — and promoting your book — online.

#32
Post Your Content to Traffic-Generating Document Sites

This is a relatively new way of creating awareness online and leaving that all-important "link bait" trail I covered earlier. In fact, I have rarely seen any other book promotion resource cover it. But it's proven to be very effective for me and many other authors.

I'm talking about a new breed of web site that stores and hosts documents.

In the early text-centric days of the Internet, articles and email were the main methods authors used to get exposure for their work. But today there are many more formats and ways to communicate stories and information, including the use of audio and video (which I'll cover in upcoming sections).

For now, I want to focus on sites that specialize in three formats in particular: Word documents, PDF files, and PowerPoint slides.

Here are four prominent sites in this category:

Scribd
www.scribd.com

SlideShare
www.slideshare.com

DocStoc
www.docstoc.com

DivShare

www.divshare.com

Why use these sites? Well, not only will all of them host your Word, PDF and PowerPoint files for free, but there are other perks too. For instance, most of them give you the ability to embed your files on your web site using user-friendly widgets that can be easily shared by you and your readers.

But the biggest benefit is that it creates yet another promotional spoke that leads to your online hub. People who visit and search these sites will find you — provided you use the right "link bait" descriptions. And, an added bonus is, these sites tend to do pretty well in Google search results.

Action step: The next time you do a presentation using a PowerPoint slide show, upload it to one or more of these sites and share it. Or take some of your text-based articles and convert them into PDF files, then post them to some of these sites, in addition to the standard article sites.

Just be sure to include your bio, a blurb about your book, and a link to your web site within the document.

Not sure how to convert files to PDF? Some newer Windows and Mac systems have build-in conversion tools. If yours doesn't, you can buy the full-blown Adobe Acrobat software for about $300. But I've been very happy using easyPDF, available for $14.95 from www.pdfonline.com/easypdf.

I bet you didn't know there were so many ways to spread your message online. And we're only getting started!

#33
Take Advantage
of Amazon.com

To completely cover Amazon.com, the behemoth of online booksellers, it would take an entire book. In fact, I've given 90-minute workshops just on the many ways you can use Amazon to promote and sell books (and much of the information was outdated just three months later). So I'm only going to hit the highlights in this section.

With that in mind, here are four primary ways you should be using Amazon.com to market your books:

1) Fill out your Public Profile

Even if you never make your books available for sale on Amazon, you should make the most of the free Public Profile that Amazon gives everyone who creates an account.

On your public profile page you can post a photo, bio, personal interests, link to your web site, and other details related to your Amazon activities. Why do this? Because any time you post a product review, a product photo, or any number of other things on the site, your name will appear with a live link to your Amazon profile. So be prepared and make it ready for visitors.

To update your Amazon profile, first create a free account at www.Amazon.com, if you don't already have one. Once you're logged in, go to "My Account," then "Personalization" and "Your Public Profile." Click "Edit Your Profile" and fill in as many sections as possible.

It's amazing how many profile pages you can go to on Amazon and find virtually nothing on them — no photo, no bio, no web site link, nothing. Don't make this mistake! Fill out yours so at least some of the millions of book consumers who visit Amazon will know who you are, what you do, and how to find you.

2) Make good use of the secret Signature field!

I refer to this as a "secret" field because most people — even those who are quite familiar with Amazon — overlook this simple but powerful element.

Look at any product review on Amazon and note what comes at the top after "By." You'll always see the reviewer's name. Sometimes you'll also find the name followed by some text in quotes. What shows in quotes is that person's Amazon "signature."

Most people use no signature at all, while some put silly descriptions such as "soccer mom" or "booklover." The best way to use a signature is to be descriptive (surprise!) and make good use of this valuable online real estate. Some authors actually put "author" as their signature. That's a good start, but you can do better.

I suggest you use either your book title or your web site as your Amazon signature.

Examples: Fred Jones "author of *The Meditation Manual*," or Fred Jones "TheMeditationManual.com."

And remember, your name and signature appear

wherever you post reviews on Amazon, which means your book title or web site will be in plain view for all to see. And if people click on your name, they are taken to your Amazon profile page, where they can learn even more about you. These are great tools, if you only use them!

To update your Amazon signature, go to "My Account," then scroll down to "Personalization." Click "Your Public Profile," then "Edit Your Profile."

3) Join Amazon's Advantage program

There are a number of ways to make your books available for sale directly from Amazon. If you go through a distributor, or have your book printed by Lightning Source, Book Locker, Lulu, Author Solutions, and other companies, they may handle that for you.

But you can make the arrangements yourself by joining Amazon's Advantage program (details at advantage.amazon.com). There's a $29.95 annual program fee (per publisher, not per title), and you must be willing to part with 55% of your book's retail price. That's right, you'll end up with 45% of the suggested retail price you set.

Reality check: Many first-time authors cry fowl over the percentage split, but come on! You'd give a distributor 55% to 60% off your cover price anyway. Amazon serves a similar function, and it reaches millions of online book buyers. So just bite the bullet and make your book available on the site.

Note that when you join the Advantage program, you must ship books to Amazon promptly in the amounts they order, which will ramp up or down as each book's sales figures warrant. It's more hands-on than having a distributor or printer handle it for you, but it's a viable option you should be aware of.

If you do join the program, be sure to upload an image of your book's cover and fill out all of the sections on your sales page, such as Editorial Reviews, Product Description, etc.

4) Give and Get Book Reviews

Amazon was one of the first sites to make significant use of user-generated reviews. And what a valuable asset they've become. Try walking into a traditional bookstore sometime and asking a clerk, "Can you tell me what the last 10 people who bought this book thought of it?" They'd think you were crazy.

But on Amazon, you can find out immediately how other people rated the book you are considering buying. It's a major factor that influences a lot of purchase decisions on the site.

So, how can you make good use of reviews?

First step: Encourage your most supportive fans to post positive reviews on your book's Amazon sales page. I believe that a person must purchase at least one item from Amazon to be able to write reviews, so not everyone will be able to randomly post their glowing testimonials. But I'm sure many of your customers have bought something from the site and have accounts there already.

Next, don't overlook the power of writing and posting your own reviews of other books. And be strategic about it. Make a list of the top 10 or 20 books you have read whose readers overlap with your own book's. Then one by one, write honest and insightful reviews of each title. After you post them, you will soon have a presence on the sales pages of other books that attract your ideal book buyer.

You can't include web site addresses within a book review, but I have gotten away with ending my reviews with "-Bob Baker, author of *Guerrilla Music Marketing Handbook*." And right at the top of the review is my name and signature: Bob Baker, "author, MusicMarketingBooks.com, FullTimeAuthor.com."

Insight: See how this works? It's not just about what happens on your own book's sales page. The idea is to have a presence *across* Amazon, in all the places where your ideal customers are already surfing!

In addition to the four tips I just covered, you should also consider:

- Creating "Listmania" lists and "So you'd like to ..." guides

- Joining Amazon's Author Central (formerly known as AmazonConnect) which allows you to link the books you've written to your profile bibliography — visit authorcentral.amazon.com for details

- Uploading product photos

- Tagging a variety of titles with keywords related to your topic

- Joining in on customer discussions

- Adding an article to Amazon's Amapedia.com

Like I said, there's a *lot* you can do on Amazon.com. We've only scratched the surface, but this gives you a solid list of ways to get started.

#34
Sell Your Book to the Ebook, Kindle, and Mobile Markets

It's been bubbling under the surface for years and debated by many people on all sides of the issue. But the verdict is now in: Electronic book sales are on the verge of a giant growth spurt.

According to a forecast published by research firm In-Stat, ebook sales worldwide will jump from $323 million in 2008 to nearly $9 billion in 2013. Of course, no one can predict the future with certainty, but there is no doubt that ebook sales are on the rise.

No, I'm not saying that paper books are going away any time soon. They'll be around for quite a while. But there are a number of developments that are making reading books on mobile devices more attractive to a growing number of consumers.

Examples: Some of the frontrunners in the ebook category are the Kindle from Amazon, the Sony Reader, and applications like Stanza (which allows people to purchase and read books on their iPhones).

Other devices competing for attention in the ebook marketplace are the iRex iLiad, Fujitsu Flepia, Hanlin eReader, Foxit eSlick Reader, Plastic Logic, Astak EZ Reader, and Jetbook.

Confused? A lot of people are, but over the coming months and years, things will get clearer as leading formats and reading devices take hold. In the meantime, don't fall asleep on the sidelines. Here are two things you can do right away to tap into the exploding ebook market:

Publish Your Books to Amazon's Digital Text Platform

Amazon has created a special place on its web site for authors and publishers to sell Kindle versions of their books. It's called the Digital Text Platform and can be found at dtp.amazon.com.

The DTP is described as "a fast and easy self-publishing tool that lets you upload and format your books for sale in the Kindle Store." I've made a few of my titles available for the Kindle. It is relatively fast and easy, but it's potentially challenging when it comes to formatting your pages.

In this current stage of ebook development, keeping things simple will save you a lot of headaches. I suggest going with text-only titles to start. Remove the images and get back to basic fonts and formatting.

Important: Something to remember with ebooks is that they can "shape shift." Most ebook devices, including the Kindle, allow users to adjust the font size on the screen. That causes page numbers to become irrelevant, so remove page numbers from your ebooks, including the Table of Contents.

The best luck I've had uploading my titles for proper Kindle formatting is creating them in a Word document, using very simple fonts and design elements, then saving it as an HTML file. Then I upload the HTML file.

Welcome to Digital Text Platform

Digital Text Platform is a fast and easy self-publishing tool that lets you upload and format your books for sale in the Kindle Store.

It's Your Thing Have a book you want to sell? Sign up with Digital Text Platform and publish your content in the Amazon Kindle Store in minutes.

Do It. If you have an Amazon.com account, you're already signed up with Digital Text Platform. Start publishing now!

Your Way. Digital Text Platform gives you everything you need to become your own publisher today. See for yourself.

 Getting Started & FAQs
Check out our quick guide and get started publishing on Amazon Kindle

 What is Amazon Kindle?
Find out what the new Amazon wireless reading device is all about.

Use Amazon's Digital Text Platform to pubish your books to the Kindle ebook format. There are no upfront costs to do so.

The cool thing about Amazon's Digital Text Platform is that you can publish anything, with or without an ISBN. Sure, you can upload and sell your entire book with the content the same as the paper version. Or you can sell sections of your book separately.

You can also sell text-based content that isn't even available in a book yet: your articles, special reports, a collection of blog posts, interview transcripts, and more.

The fine print: Amazon takes an even bigger chunk of the action with its Kindle Store. You'll get 35% of the suggested retail price you set. Yes, that means Amazon keeps 65%. That's a lot, but being there will probably help you reach a lot of buyers you wouldn't otherwise.

Use Smashwords to Convert and Sell Your Book in Multiple Ebook Formats

If all this ebook formatting business sounds confusing, there's a site that may very well be a godsend to cure what ails you. It's called Smashwords and can be found at www.smashwords.com.

Action step: Go to Smashwords, start a free account, and download its free *Smashwords Style Guide* at smashwords.com/books/view/52. It will spell out how to format your ebook documents for best results.

Smashwords allows authors and publishers to upload as many documents as they want. The site then runs each title through its online "meatgrinder" and converts your single document into multiple ebook and digital formats, including epub, Sony Reader (LRF), Kindle (.mobi), Palm Doc (PDB), PDF, rich text file (RTF), and plain text, as well as into online HTML and Javascript formats.

And Smashwords does this all for free! They make money only when you send your customers to the Smashwords site to purchase your ebook titles directly from them. They keep 15% of every sale and send you the remaining 85%. Sounds pretty sweet.

Tip: If you're already selling PDF ebook downloads from your own site, you should probably keep doing that. But for all of the other ebook formats you don't want to mess with, it might be a good idea to send your customers to your sales pages at Smashwords.

This is a newer site that I'm sure will evolve a lot over time. It seems to be adding new features all the time. Visit www.smashwords.com/about for details.

#35
Get Widespread Exposure With Online Press Releases

In a recent workshop, I showed a PowerPoint slide that proclaimed, "Press Releases: They're not just for journalists anymore!" It's true. Let me explain …

Traditionally speaking, press releases are written announcements that are sent to editors, journalists, and talk show producers. The goal of sending a press release is to grab the attention of media people so they write about you or book you as a guest on their show. Press releases still serve that function today. And they can be delivered in many ways: by snail mail, fax, email, and more.

History: As the Internet became more popular, some smart companies began offering electronic press release delivery. They'd send your release, or a link to it, by email to their list of targeted media people.

Next came sites that posted press releases on public web sites — like online repositories of the latest news. Some of these sites charged a fee, but many came along that offered press release posting for free.

Then an interesting thing happened. Promoters noticed that their press release pages were showing up in search engine results and on niche topic sites that published news "feeds." And it became apparent that consumers and everyday people were finding the online press releases even more than journalists.

Which brings us back to my opening proclamation: "Press Releases: They're not just for journalists anymore!"

Lesson: Get it out of your head that the only reason to write and post a press release is to get the attention of a media person. These days, you should think of online press releases as another tentacle in your Internet "presence" toolbox (pardon the mixed metaphors). So write them with consumers, as well as journalists, in mind.

Here's a list of nine press release web sites. Some offer free postings, others offer paid services, and some offer both.

24-7 PressRelease.com
www.24-7pressrelease.com

Free Press Release
www.free-press-release.com

i-Newswire
www.i-newswire.com

Marketwire
www.marketwire.com

PR Leap
www.prleap.com

PR Log
www.prlog.org

PR Newswire
www.prnewswire.com

PR Web
www.prweb.com

Pressbox

www.pressbox.co.uk

There's a lot of advice out there about how to properly format a press release and finesse it in ways that make it more likely to be noticed and "picked up" by the media. Again, we're not concerned about attracting journalists only, but there are some PR rules that apply to book consumers too.

Hot tip: The best press releases are generally not about you or your book! That's right. As I've emphasized before, the focus should always be on the reader and his or her interests.

So if you are promoting your new book about how to improve your bowling score, your first instinct might be to write a press release headline such as:

"Fred Jones Publishes New Book on Bowling"

But that would be wrong!

A better headline for your press release would be:

"5 Easy Ways to Add 50 Points to Your Bowling Score This Week"

Do you know why it's better? Because the second headline is more likely to get a response from your target audience. It speaks to their wants and desires directly. And once you get them reading you're great tips, they'll learn about your book and be more likely to buy it!

#36
Submit Your Book
to These Review Sites

Book reviews used to be one of the primary ways that publishers got exposure for new books. Don't get me wrong, it's still quite valuable and should be pursued. But these days, in my opinion, reviews are just a small part of your overall marketing arsenal.

In years past, everyone wanted to get their book reviewed in the major media — from the *New York Times* and *Wall Street Journal* to the local metropolitan daily newspaper. There was a lot of competition, which lead to limited opportunities for independent authors and self-publishers

Good news: Today, the definition of "media exposure" has greatly expanded. There are now thousands of web sites and blogs that review books. You should send your books to the most relevant sites in this category.

Here are six review sites that are receptive to independent publishers:

Midwest Book Review
www.midwestbookreview.com/get_rev.htm

ForeWord Magazine
www.forewordmagazine.com/reviews/guidelines.aspx

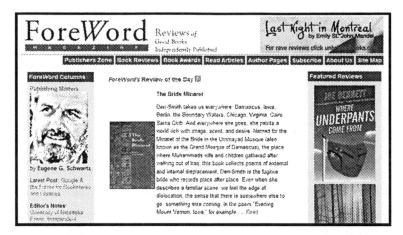

ForewordMagazine.com is one of many sites that reviews books from independent authors and publishers.

Rain Taxi
www.raintaxi.com/publisher.shtml

Book Ideas
www.bookideas.com/about/getreviewed.cfm

The Modern Word
www.themodernword.com/submissions.html

BookReview.com
www.bookreview.com/publishers2.htm

Hot tip: To find targeted review sites, do a Google search for "genre book reviews." Replace the word genre with your topic, i.e. "mystery book reviews" or "business book reviews."

Happy book review site hunting!

37

Promote Your Author Events on These Sites

This is where the real world meets the virtual world. Yes, you can and should use the Internet to promote your book signings, workshops, and other live events. The reverse is also true: You should use your live appearances to drive traffic to your web site.

Visit the appropriate sites below to promote your live events for free online:

BookTour.com
www.booktour.com/readers/adding_events

Authors and Experts – Book Signing Calendar
www.authorsandexperts.com/calendar_form.php

EventCaster
www.netread.com/calendar

Upcoming
upcoming.yahoo.com

Eventful
www.eventful.com

CraigsList
www.craigslist.org

Locus Online: Author Appearances
www.locusmag.com/AuthorEventsByAuthor.html

#38
Take Advantage of These Three Free Google Services

Yes, Google is the undisputed king of search. But it's also a global technology factory that is constantly churning out new tools and resources — most of which are free.

In this section I will focus on three Google services you should be using to promote your books online: Google Book Search, Google Base, and Google Knol.

Google Book Search

books.google.com

Even though there's been some controversy over the Google Book Search service, the site makes it sound pretty tempting:

"Promote Your Books on Google — for free ... We respect the tremendous creative effort you put into your books. That's why we want to make it as easy as possible for people to find them."

Scroll to the bottom of the page and click "Information for Publishers." That will take you to a page that explains the program and how to submit your titles.

Here's a taste of how Google explains it:

"We scan the full text of your book because we want people to be able to search all its content. But users can only access a limited number of pages to

Use Google Knol to share your expertise with the world.

determine whether they've found what they're looking for.

"We understand that your books are valuable, so we treat them with special care. All the books you send us will be hosted on Google servers and protected by the same security as Google.com's search data.

"To further protect your book content, printing and image copying functions are disabled on all Google Book Search pages."

My opinion: Don't worry about people stealing your stuff. Do everything you can to help readers find it. And Google Book Search can do some of that for you.

Google Base

www.google.com/base

To me, Google Base is a little like Craig's List and Ebay combined. According to the site:

"Google Base is a free Google service that helps you publish virtually any kind of information — be it your latest riveting screenplay or a listing for your slightly dented 1989 Honda Accord."

You can post events, jobs, things for sale, and ... products, including books. All for free!

Google Knol

knol.google.com

If I had to describe Google Knol, it would be "Wikipedia.org meets EzineArticles.com." According to Google: "Knol makes it easy for you to write and share your knowledge with the world."

You've written a book. You have knowledge to share. Why not share some of it on Google Knol?

39

Reach Out to Other Authors and Experts

This is one of the smartest things you can do, and sady, most authors don't even think of it as an option. In fact, they often shy away from or avoid other authors out of fear of mingling with "the competition."

My advice: Dump that misguided notion and move on!

In the early days of my publishing career, I created a mental barrier that plagues many novice authors. I separated "them" from "me." I built an imaginary wall that unknowingly kept me from enjoying some valuable opportunities.

"They" were the successful authors in my field — the writers who inspired me and influenced my style, or who I simply looked up to and aspired to emulate. The only problem was, I put "them" at a distance. And not just at a physical distance; I also put them on a mental level that was "outside my league."

Thankfully, at some point, I took chances and started reaching out to other authors and experts by email and phone. In the 1990s, I found an email address for Jay Conrad Levinson in an online forum. Jay is the creator of the *Guerrilla Marketing* series of books and someone who greatly influenced my music marketing ideas early on.

So I sent Jay an email, not expecting to hear back from him. But later that same day, I did! A few years later, Jay gave me a great cover blurb for my *Branding Yourself Online* book. And in 2008 I became an official *Guerrilla* author when I contributed a chapter to the book *Guerrilla Marketing on the Front Lines*. That email I sent him years ago proved to be priceless!

Another example: Several years ago I read an article in *Inc.* magazine about creativity in the workplace. One of the people quoted in the article was Arthur VanGundy, author of *108 Ways to Get a Bright Idea (and Increase Your Creative Potential)*. I was so thrilled by what he said, I gathered my courage and called the university where he worked. Within minutes I was speaking with him on the phone.

With these early wins to boost my confidence, I started reaching out even more to other authors and experts. Jack Canfield, Joe Vitale, Seth Godin, Chris Anderson, Daniel Pink, Mitch Meyerson, Marcia Yudkin, David Meerman Scott, Greg Godin, John Kremer, and Dan Poynter are just some of the authors I've corresponded with over the years via email, phone, and in person.

Reality: Not everyone will respond to your emails and phone calls. But I bet you'll be surprised by the number that do reply. And these relationships can be extremely fruitful. Some will simply thrill you because you have connected with someone you admire; while others will develop into greater business and personal relationships.

So ... grow beyond "me vs. them" thinking. Start reaching out to your favorite authors today!

40

Find New Connections with Advanced Google Searches

One of the funniest web sites I've seen lately is LetMeGoogleThatForYou.com. Its purpose: "This is for all those people who find it more convenient to bother you with their question rather than Google it for themselves."

I know the feeling. I've lost count of the number of times someone has asked me a question like, "What's the best way to learn HTML?" More often than not, when I ask, "Have you tried searching Google?" the reply is, "Well, um ... no."

So, just in case this has escaped you, there's a world of information at your fingertips, if you only go to a search site like Google and seek it out.

But that's just a starting point. Doing a quick search for something is one thing. But knowing a few advanced insider tricks can help you discover more and richer finds on the Internet. Here are my top four advanced searching techniques:

1) Use variations on keyword phrases

Let's say you want to compile a list of sites that might review your book on dog grooming. Of course, you can go to Google and enter "dog grooming" into the search field.

Then, one by one, you visit the web pages that

come up in the search results. You would then bookmark or in some way compile a list of the most promising sites. Job well done, right?

Not so fast!

Go back and also search for variations and alternate pharses related to dog grooming, such as: dog grooming tips, dog grooming training, nail clipping dogs, brushing dogs hair, keep your dog clean, etc. Each phrase will bring a different set of search results. So don't stop after the first or second search.

2) Use quotation marks

Google has some pretty cool advanced features. One of the simplest involves the use of quotation marks. Let me explain: In a normal search, such as the previous dog grooming example, Google returns pages that display the words "dog" and "grooming" anywhere on the page. That's fine, but you will have sites turn up that have nothing to do with canine hygene.

When you put quotation marks around a phrase in the search field, Google will give you only pages that use those words together in that order. Therefore, the results are more likely to be accurate matches for what you're looking for. If you don't do this already, start using quotation marks to fine-tune your searches.

3) Use the "link" search function

To the right of the normal Google search box you'll see a small link that says "Advanced Search." If you've never clicked it, please do, because there you'll find a lot of useful search options. And once on that

Find web pages that have...
- all these words:
- this exact wording or phrase:
- one or more of these words:

Advanced Search

Page-specific tools:
- Find pages similar to the page: Search
- Find pages that link to the page: Search

Google's advanced search features allow you to dig deeper and find more of what you're looking for online.

---

page, be sure to click "Date, usage rights, numeric range, and more" for two of my favorite Google search tricks.

Under "Page-specific tools," you'll find a box with the description "Find pages similar to the page." How do you use this feature? Let's say you just discovered AlohaMagazine.com, and it's the ideal type of site to promote your new *History of Hula Dancing* book. If you could just find more web sites similar to that one, you'd be in hula heaven.

You see where I'm going with this. Just enter www.AlohaMagazine.com into that "similar to" field and you'll find other sites like it.

Quick tip: There's a faster way to access this Google feature. Just enter the word "related," a colon, and then the web address into the regular search box, as in "related:www.AlohaMagazine.com" — no need to use the quotes; I just did that to set them apart.

4) Use the "related" search function

Finally, one of my favorite advanced Google search techniques: The "Find pages that link to the page" option, which will reveal pages that link *to* any page or site you enter. How is this one helpful?

If you write novels that would appeal to fans of John Grisham, you can quickly hunt down sites that link to Grisham's by entering "link:www.jgrisham.com" into the regular search box (again, without the quotes). This trick alone can uncover online book exposure gold.

The next time you wonder where you should focus your Internet book marketing efforts, use these advanced search features to find exactly the right web sites for you and your book.

#41
Run Paid Advertising Sparingly, if at All

I'll be honest with you. I've spent very little money on paid advertsing throughout my entire career as an author. In the early days, it was out of necessity — I didn't have a budget for it at all. But as my business has grown, paid ads have remained low on my list of effective ways to promote and sell books.

Other authors and publishers report the same results. Paid ads aren't all that effective, unless you run them repeatedly for months and years on end in the right places. Believe me, there are better ways to invest your limited resources.

Reality: Paid ads are the very last thing I recommend, but they are often the first thing that novice promoters think of when it comes to marketing. That's why this is the only section in this book that will even remotely cover this topic.

If you're going to engage in some form of paid advertising, be smart about it. Use the most affordable methods and be strategic in your approach.

Strategy: One online advertsing option you might consider is something called "pay per click." The name says it all: Your small line ad appears on various web sites, and you are only charged when someone clicks on it. Most of the pay-per-click programs also let you set a limit on how much you want to spend each month. When you reach that amount — whether it's $10 or $5,000 — your ads stop running until the start of the next month. This is a nice option for self-promoting authors with small budgets.

The most popular pay-per-click program is Google AdWords. When you do a Google search, the results that appear in the wide column on the left are considered the "natural" or "organic" search results. Those little line ads that appear in the thin right column (and sometimes at the very top) and are labeled "Sponsored Links" are the pay-per-click ads.

Your goal is to come up in the organic search results on the left. But the next best thing is showing up among the Google AdWords listings, which you pay for using a bidding system. In essence, the more you are willing to pay per click, the higher your ad will appear in the column.

Yahoo, Microsoft and many other companies offer pay-per-click ad programs. Here are some links to help you research your options:

Google AdWords
adwords.google.com

Yahoo Search Marketing
searchmarketing.yahoo.com

Microsoft adCenter
adcenter.microsoft.com

Facebook Advertising
www.facebook.com/advertising

BidVertiser
www.bidvertiser.com

There are entire books written about how to run effective pay-per-click campaigns. It is an art and a science. Read a book like *Pay Per Click Search Engine Marketing for Dummies* and do your homework before jumping into this paid ad arena.

Another option: As you should know by now, my philosophy is all about targeting. You need to go directly to your ideal readers and fans with your message. So if you must scratch the itch to spend money on ads, *go for quality over quantity*.

If there is a blog, web site, podcast, or email newsletter that reaches the ideal consumer for your book, contact the person who runs the site and see if they will accept a small fee from you each month in exchange for a sponsorship of some kind.

Better yet: Barter for the placement! If you have decent web traffic or a few thousand ezine subscribers, offer to swap exposure to each other's audiences. That way, you both win, and you don't have to spend a penny on advertsing.

Again, go the paid advertising route only if you feel you absolutely have to. Believe me, it is not the miracle cure for obscurity.

But if you do use it, keep your ad budget low and your message targeted to the exact types of people you need to be reaching online.

Next up: We demystify social networking and Web 2.0 marketing.

Making the Most of Social Media and Web 2.0

#42
Understand What "Social Networking" Really Is

Is your head spinning with thoughts of Facebook, Twitter, MySpace, YouTube, Technorati, Digg, and all these new "social networking" web sites?

Well, relax. This section will put things in perspective and make it all easier to understand. Looked at in a different light, social networking isn't so mysterious after all.

First, let's address the terms. The phrase "social networking" is simply a reference to the way people are interacting and communicating with each other online. That's all.

And the related phrase "social media" is just a way of describing all the multi-sensory online tools (text, audio, images, video, widgets, applications) that people are using to be "social."

Another odd phrase you hear a lot is "Web 2.0." But don't worry. It's not a new software version of the Internet you have to upgrade to.

Definition: Web 2.0 is a term coined by O'Reilly Media, a computer book publisher that hosts an annual conference by that name. Web 2.0 is simply a way of describing a more interactive Internet, which evolved out of the static web sites of the past.

Even if you know all of this already, you may still

be confused and overwhelmed by all there is to learn to promote your book effectively online. Again, relax. You don't have to know it all on Day One. Chip away at the learning curve and absorb it little by little.

What's Really Going On Under the Hood?

When it comes to technological advances, you must remember one thing: Your focus should not be on the tools and the gadgets themselves. Your attention must stay on what's powering the technology. And the fuel that runs all of these electronic and digital systems is ... *people*.

That's right. Plain old human beings.

So, wrapping your head around "social network-ing" all boils down to understanding people. And here's the rock-bottom secret to it all:

Human beings are social creatures, and they have been for centuries. For generations, people have gathered in groups: The tribe, the town square, the corner bar, the family reunion, the gang at work, the sports team, the church picnic ... you name it.

People have a primal need to be around and communicate with other people — especially with those who share their outlook, interests and values. It's easy to get bogged down with ever-changing tech tools and file formats, but when you look under the hood, you'll see something that never changes: human nature at work.

Insight: Think of our basic need to communicate with each other as a body of water. It flows when and where it can. In the past, people were limited by geography and distance. You could only congregate with people in your immediate vicinity, unless you made the effort to travel to other places. Of course, in more recent decades, people made good use of snail mail and the telephone to connect, too. But ...

The Internet makes it possible to huddle up with like-minded people worldwide — without leaving home. Blogs, podcasts and video streams are simply the latest tools that allow people to express themselves and make connections with others — but now they're able to do so across the globe.

What an exciting time to be alive!

Truth: Ideas flow regardless, but technology gives people more powerful options to share their messages with other humans.

So focus on the people aspect of this Internet marketing thing at all times. You have important ideas to deliver with your book. There are people around the globe who need to hear what you have to say. Social media sites and Web 2.0 tools are the new pipelines to get that message delivered!

#43
Become a Consumer
of the Technology First

Countless times I've had conversations with impatient authors that go something like this ...

"Bob, I'm going to start my own blog soon and I really want to know how to use it to sell more books. What should I do?"

"Well," I reply, "what blogs do you subscribe to and read now?"

"Umm ..." he or she says, befuddled. "Actually, I don't read any. I've just heard that I should do one."

I understand their eagerness to jump into the online marketing waters. But when you think about it, this is backwards thinking.

Question: Would someone try to direct a film without ever having watched one? Or would an actor go audition for a play without ever having experienced live theatre?

Of course not. That would be like trying to write a book without ever having read one!

Most likely, the thing that motivated you to write a book was your consumption of other books. At some point you said, "I also have a story that needs to be told. I could write a book too." And as you started to transform your ideas into words, you may have found yourself influenced by your favorite writers' styles.

And that's a good thing. We all have people we admire who color how we approach a new craft until we find our own style and voice. The same thing is true of embracing new marketing tools and technologies.

Key: If you want to become a blogger, start reading what other bloggers are doing. First, look through the Technorati Top 100 Blogs list at www.technorati.com/pop/blogs and subscribe to a few or more. Also read the most prominent blogs in your field to see how your topic is currently being covered.

Once you do this for a while, you'll soon develop preferences and opinions. "I like the tone of her blog. He's too much of a self-promoter. That one is boring. Oh, I like that idea." Before long you'll formulate a solid idea of how you want your blog to look and feel.

Tip: This "become a consumer first" idea doesn't apply only to blogs. Take this same approach with podcasts, audio and video content, social networking sites, and more.

Yes, it takes a little more time to get acquainted with the landscape this way. But you'll be a much better informed and more effective author if you become a consumer first, and a self-promoter second.

#44
Participate in Discussion Forums, Groups and Mailing Lists

To make the most of online social networking, you must be willing to be "social" and to "network." Again, this isn't about digital technology; it's all about human beings communicating with each other. And on the Internet, there are millions of conversations taking place at any given moment. As an author, you should be joining in on some of that dialogue.

There are myriad ways to interact online, and we'll cover many of them in upcoming sections. But the best place to start is with discussion forums, groups and mailing lists — forms of Internet communication that have been in existence for many years and are still used extensively today.

This category of the social web basically has three formats:

1) Discussions that take place on a web page, where participants can view and respond to a topic thread,

2) Individual messages that are emailed to all "members" of the mailing list forum,

3) Or forums that combine both the web site and email components.

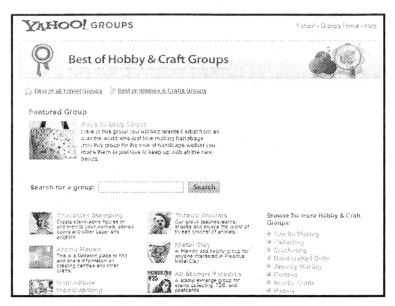

On community sites like Yahoo! Groups you can find thousands of discussion groups on every topic imaginable.

Two of the most popular sites that host such forums are:

Yahoo! Groups

groups.yahoo.com

Google Groups

groups.google.com

Go to either one of them and search for existing groups dedicated to hundreds of topics.

It's time to return to a familiar mantra: You must not concern yourself with the vast majority of these forums. Your only goal is to find groups that are in alignment with your book and message. And there are plenty of them, no matter what your topic.

For instance, there are forums and mailing lists for

pharmacists, inventors, midwives, Mozilla software developers, Canadian nursing students, German translators, Scottish people who stutter, butch-femmes, Poicephalus Parrot owners, and more.

With this amazing diversity of online discussion, certainly there's a group out there for you!

To test this idea, I looked up discussion forums related to tango dancing, and quickly found the following:

Argentine Tango
tangoconnections.ning.com

Tango Forum
topix.com/forum/music/tango

Tango Zone
groups.yahoo.com/group/atangozone

Tango-L Mailing List
pythia.uoregon.edu/~llynch/Tango-L/

Dance Forums - Tango Argentino
dance-forums.com

There really is something out there for practically everyone.

The best way to make the most of these forums is to periodically check in and either start a topic or add to an existed discussion thread.

Important: Don't just post blatant "Hey, check out my book" remarks. Your goal is to truly add something useful to the discussion — even if it's only a short comment. Then include a blurb at the end as your "signature," such as:

Fred Jones

Author of The Complete Guide to Feeding
and Caring for Your Poicephalus Parrot

www.ParrotGuide.com

Tip: Being active on these forums can be time
consuming, so be sure to identity the most potent
ones. Pick two or three groups that are highly
targeted and have an active membership, and place
your efforts on them. That way, you'll become a
recognized authority to people who really matter.

#45
Tap Into the Blogosphere Goldmine

Here's a quick primer on blogs and how you can use them to promote your book ...

As you may know, the word blog is short for "web log." A blog is basically an online journal that its author uses to publish "posts," which are separate entries to the journal. The term "blogosphere" merely refers to the ever-expanding collection of blogs across the Internet.

Blogs can be published for any reason and subject matter imaginable. From teenagers and activists to politicians and best-selling authors, anyone can easily and inexpensively publish a blog.

In many ways, blogs are just another version of a web site with multiple pages. You can visit and read a blog page in the same way you do any other web page. The main thing that sets a blog apart from a basic web page is a nifty web-based file format called RSS.

Definition: RSS stands for Really Simple Syndication. In general, it is used to publish and organize frequently updated digital content, such as blogs, news feeds, and podcasts. The coolest thing about RSS is that it gives people the ability to *subscribe* to blogs and podcasts.

Feeding the RSS Monster

In the old days, when you found a web site you were interested in and wanted to stay on top of, you had two choices:

1) subscribe to the site's ezine (if it offered one) and get updates by email, or ...

2) bookmark the site by adding it to your browser's favorites list (but you had to remember to visit it in the future).

In essence, an RSS feed allows you to subscribe to a web site, which just happens to be a blog. You can subscribe to blogs using something called a news reader, feed reader, or aggregator.

These readers are popping up everywhere. The latest versions of the Firefox and Internet Explorer browsers allow you to subscribe to feeds directly from the browser. You can also subscribe if you have a personalized page set up on Google, Yahoo or AOL. Or you can use programs and sites such as Bloglines, FeedDemon, and more.

Perspective: If you're not familiar with how these feed readers work, think about how your email Inbox operates. You open your email program and up pops all of your latest incoming emails, listed by subject line, with the most recent message at the top.

Feed readers work in a similar way. Open it up, and all of the blogs you subscribe to will show up, with the latest content at the top, usually with just the headline and maybe the first few lines of the blog post displaying. It's a pretty convenient way to have only the information you want delivered to your desktop computer, laptop, or even your cell phone.

Find Blogs That Cater to Your Audience

Later we'll cover publishing your own blog. For now, let's focus on getting as much exposure as possible for your book on other people's existing blogs. The first thing you should do is track down the blogs that are already attracting your ideal readers.

Here are the two best blog directories to start your search:

Technorati Blog Directory
technorati.com/blogs/directory

Google Blog Search
blogsearch.google.com

Search both sites for words, phrases, and topics related to your book. Once you've compiled a list of targeted blogs, here are some simple things you can start doing right away:

- **Leave comments**. Most blogs allow you to post comments about each entry, and those comments do get read. Don't misuse this feature with "comment spam" that mindlessly hypes your book. Make sure your comment adds to or amplifies some aspect of the blog author's post. It's okay to make a sensible reference to your book within your comment. At the end, put your name and a link to your web site.

- **Send useful ideas and links to blog authors**. One of your new online marketing goals should be to network with and get to know bloggers. Search your favorite blogs for a Contact or About link that includes the email address of the blogger. Store these names and addresses in a database, then occasionally send them compliments, links to sites that might interest them, or news about something you are working on. Reaching out to bloggers in this way will strengthen relationships with them and lead to some nice online exposure.

Uncover Blog Gold With Blogrolls

The term "blogroll" refers to a list of other blogs that bloggers recommend. You'll often find them in the right-hand column of your favorite blogs. Not every blog features them, but the ones that do can be very helpful in your hunt for the perfect blogs.

The reason they are so useful: Blogrolls act as filters that will save you time when researching and identifying blogs that cater to your topic. For instance, if you go to the Music Industry Report blog at www.MusicIndustryReport.org, you'll find links to a couple dozen of the best music business related blogs, including mine. If this was your subject, this list would be invaluable.

So when you find a well-read blog that ideally covers your topic, look to see if it features a blogroll and investigate those sites next. And if the best blogs on that list have blogrolls too … you get the picture. Blogrolls can be great research tools.

#46
Promote Via Podcasts and Online Radio Shows

Author Andrew Darlow says that getting exposure on podcasts has been one of the most effective ways he has promoted his book, *301 Inkjet Tips and Techniques*.

"I've seen a big boost in email newsletter subscriptions and book sales after I've appeared on certain podcasts and online radio shows that are related in some way to my book's topic," Darlow says. "I think podcast listeners are a great target audience because they have taken the time to research, download, and listen to a show on a specific topic in which they are interested."

What You Need to Know About Podcasts

Now that we're comfortable with blogs and RSS feeds, let's dig into this phenomenon called podcasting. Even though the name was inspired by Apple's iPod, you don't need an iPod to either produce or listen to a podcast.

Definition: In essence, a podcast is an audio blog that features links to MP3 files (and even video content). A podcast can include music or spoken-word content and often features both. Think of it as a radio show that anyone with the right tools can produce and broadcast to the world.

Using the same RSS feed technology as blogs, people can subscribe to their favorite podcasts using a "podcatcher," a program that automatically downloads the latest media files from a selected list of podcasts to the subscriber's computer. Some popular pod-catchers include iTunes, Odeo, PodNova, and Juice.

Promoting Your Book Through Other People's Podcasts

As you did with blogs, the first thing to do is uncover the best podcasts and online radio shows for your book's topic. Here are some places to start your search:

Podcast Pickle
www.podcastpickle.com

Podcast Alley
www.podcastalley.com

iTunes
www.apple.com/itunes/store/podcasts.html

Odeo
www.odeo.com

Okay. You're now armed with a hot list of podcasts that cater to your target audience. Now what? Here are my top four podcast promotion ideas:

- **Send review copies of your book**. If a podcast or online radio show seems ideally in line with the topic of your book, send the host a review copy. If the Contact or About page includes a physical address, you can just blindly mail a copy. But it would be even better to email the

Podcast directories like PodcastPickle.com can help you find shows that cover your topic and attract your ideal fans.

host and ask if you can send one. That way there's an expectation that your book is on the way. Even if the host never reviews books, he or she might reference it, or better yet, invite you to be a guest. Which leads us to …

- **Offer yourself as a guest**. If the podcast features a talk-show format, especially one that includes guests, present yourself as the ideal interview candidate. Often it's as simple as sending an email to the show host with a short bio and a pitch for why your topic is worth covering. Be sure to offer a free review copy or link to the ebook version of your title. Emailing a teaser list of bullet point topics or suggested questions wouldn't hurt either.

- **Submit audio comments**. In the previous blog section, I suggested that you leave intelligent comments. You can leave text comments on many podcast sites too. But a more creative option would be to record and send an audio response to something a podcaster covered on a recent episode. Just record it using your computer or a digital audio recorder and send an MP3 (or email a link to your audio file). Many podcasters will appreciate you giving them extra content to include in their shows, and you'll benefit accordingly.

- **Record podcast show IDs**. You've heard these on commercial radio for decades. Well, they translate easily to the podcast world as well. Your recording would go something like this: "This is Dave Smith, author of *The History of Hula Dancing*, and you're listening to my favorite show, the Island Paradise Podcast." Easy, huh?

We'll cover more on how to create and publish your own audio content in an upcoming section. For now, just know that existing podcasts and online radio shows offer potent ways to spread your message and increase book sales.

#47
Tap Into Book-Specific Social Sites

By now you know that you must get exposure in the places where your ideal readers are hanging out online. We've already covered blogs, podcasts, and discussion forums. But there's another breed of interactive web site you should be aware of: those that attract book lovers in general.

Believe it or not, not everyone reads books on a regular basis. So if you can find online destinations that cater to lots of book enthusiasts — people who love to read — you can't go wrong.

Here are nine such sites worth exploring:

AuthorsDen

www.authorsden.com

Described as a "vibrant free online literary community of authors and readers," this site boasts more than one million visitors a month. Authors are encouraged to interact with readers and post info on their books, events, articles, and more.

BookCrossing

www.bookcrossing.com

This unusual site encourages its 750,000-plus members to read books and pass them on, sometimes leaving them in public places to be discovered by strangers. Each reader logs the book's journey across the country and around the world.

BookGlutton

www.bookglutton.com

This site serves as an online book club designed for people to share and discuss ebooks.

Booksprouts

www.booksprouts.com

Another site where you can start a book club or reading group and discuss your favorite titles.

FiledBy

www.filedby.com

A site that provides authors with free pages to promote their books and interact with readers.

GoodReads

www.goodreads.com

A web site where members publicly share their reading lists, reviews, ratings, and book recommendations.

LibraryThing

www.librarything.com

A site with 700,000 members who share and discuss the books they love.

Listal

www.listal.com

A place to list, rate, tag, and review books, music, movies, games, and more.

BookSprouts.com is an online destination for people interested in reading groups. It's one of many sites that attracts book lovers.

Shelfari

www.shelfari.com

Another popular online community of book lovers who share their reading lists and opinions.

Hot tip: Your first instinct may be to introduce your book to these communities and get them discussing your title. That's a good idea, and you should definitely explore that. But there's a much better way to ease into these book-specific social networking sites ...

Make a list of the top 10 books that you like which are similar to yours. Search for established groups already discussing these titles. Join in the conversation and subtly make them aware that you are an author.

Do you think these targeted book lovers might be interested in your book too?

#48
Make Fabulous Friends with Facebook

How would you like to be part of a social networking site used by nearly one-fifth of all Internet users on the planet? That's the clout that Facebook.com can boast. Not bad for a site founded in 2004 by a few Harvard students who wanted to create a new way to interact with their friends.

There's a good chance you're already on Facebook. If not, you really should sign up for a free account ... today! If you are on Facebook, there's a good chance you're not using the site to its full potential to promote and sell your book.

Note that a full discussion on how to use this one site alone could take up volumes, so I'll only scratch the surface here. With that in mind, here are the top five Facebook features you should be using to promote your book:

1) Personal Profile

This is the first step for everyone who joins Facebook. So if you're just getting started, spend some time beefing up your profile. Definitely upload an appealing profile photo, then fill out the sections under "personal information."

Include details about your book and it's subject matter. Under "favorite books," include lots of references to similar titles. You can list more than one web site, so if you have separate addresses for your author site, blog, Amazon author page, and so on, list them all.

Once your Facebook profile is in good shape, invite your friends and family to "friend" you, of course. Then take advantage of the feature that allows Facebook to access your email and search for people you know who are current members. Beyond that, promote your profile link to your previous customers and email list, as well as on your web site.

Key: Even if someone is already on your email list or following you in some other way, you want them to connect with you on Facebook too. It's all about repetition and giving your readers lots of ways to stay in touch with you.

2) Fan Page

The people who run Facebook are not dummies. They realized that a lot of members were using the site to promote themselves. So they created a special type of page for business purposes called Facebook Pages. To learn more about them, scroll to the very bottom of any Facebook page and click on "Advertising." Then find a link at the top that says "Pages." But don't worry, starting a business page (also called a Fan Page) costs nothing.

The main advantage to starting a separate fan page for yourself as an author is the ability to send updates to all of your fans at once, no matter how many fans you have. With a personal profile, you can send messages to only 20 people at a time. (This is Facebook's way of keeping spammers from bulk

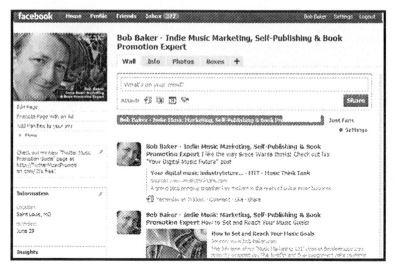

On Facebook, I have both a personal profile and a Fan Page (pictured above). It's a good idea to have both.

mailing thousands of people at one time.)

Another perk: With a personal profile, you can have no more than 5,000 friends. That's not a problem for most people, but if you're a popular author, you'll disappoint a lot of your fans when you reach your limit. With a business/fan page, there is no cap on the number of fans you can have. That's why I recommend having both a personal profile and a fan page on Facebook.

3) Groups

Here's another great interactive feature on Facebook: the ability to create forums dedicated to specific topics. There are two ways to use the Groups function. One is to seek out existing groups that are attracting the type of people who might enjoy your book. Example: A search for "Harry Potter" brought up many groups, one with more than 33,000 members.

But perhaps the best thing to do is start a Facebook group around the topic of your book. In fact, if it's fitting, use the book title as the group name and your book cover for the group image. Just make sure the group exists to foster lively discussions surrounding the book's topic, not just to serve as a place to post sales pitches.

Encourage members to start discussions or post questions and invite replies. Again, the purpose is to get people involved in your topic or genre, while gently making them aware that you are an authority and an author with a book for sale.

4) Events

When you do readings, workshops, or book signings, Facebook is a great place to make people aware of your live events. To create an event listing, look to the bottom left of your browser window while on any Facebook page and click the little red calendar icon that has a 31 in it. Next, click the "Create an Event" button at the top right.

Then just fill out all the event details: date, time, location, address, description, etc. Once your event is created, you can invite people on your friends list to attend. One cool feature Facebook offers is the ability to filter the people you invite by their location — so, for example, you can select just everyone on your friends list who lives in Chicago and invite them only.

Tip: You can also use Facebook to invite people to virtual events such as teleclasses and online trainings.

Just type something like "Anywhere from your phone" or "Anywhere you have access to a computer" in the Location field.

5) Applications

One thing there's no shortage of on Facebook is the number of gizmos, games and applications you can add to your profile and share with your friends. While a lot of these things can be fun, I encourage you to be very strategic as you choose which ones to add and use. You can "throw sheep" at people and send silly quizzes, but always ask yourself "Why?"

Important: The best applications serve a purpose! They engage your audience or pull in useful content that otherwise resides outside of Facebook. Apps that pull in your videos or still pictures from YouTube or Flickr are good ones. Also, if you can integrate your activity on Twitter or your blog using an app, that's worth considering.

Idea: There are a number of book applications designed for users to show off their favorite books. Hmm, I wonder how you might put these to use? Of course, by using one to highlight your book! If you have audio versions of your writings or you simply enjoy expressing yourself via spoken word, there are several popular music apps you can use to share your audio content.

To search for specific types of Facebook applications, look to the bottom left of any page and click the "Applications" link.

As I mentioned, this section only briefly touches on how you can use Facebook to promote and sell books. The main thing to know is that Facebook is big and growing bigger every month. So stay active on the site as you make new friends and turn many of them into fans.

#49
Use Twitter to Tweet Your Message to the Masses

You've no doubt heard of Twitter, one of the fastest growing social sites going in recent years. It's often referred to as a "micro-blogging" platform because of the minimalist nature of how people use it — to post short messages of no more than 140 characters long (including spaces). The messages can be sent, received and read on cell phones and regular computers via special applications or the Twitter web site.

Messages you post to Twitter are referred to as "tweets." You can keep track of tweets posted by people you choose to "follow." Likewise, people who want to track your activities can do so by clicking the "follow" button on your Twitter profile page.

Twitter is by far the easiest and quickest way to get involved in social networking. It takes minutes to set up an account, upload a photo, and add a short bio and a link to your web site. And, with a 140-character maximum, it takes no time to craft a message to post. In fact, you'll spend more time editing your thoughts down to one or two quick sentences than you will thinking of something to say.

The site was originally created to help its users answer that probing question, "What are you doing?" For better or worse, many users have taken this theme to heart by letting others know everything they're doing — and I mean *everything*! Common messages report such meaningful activities as "Stopping to get gas and buy a pack of cigs" or "Running late for the photo shoot" or "It's raining outside and I'm bored."

In a blog post I wrote some years ago shortly after joining Twitter, I wrote, "You're bored? Try reading through this mountain of trivial Twitter updates. Then you'll know what true agony is!"

Is Twitter Worth the Time?

That's the most common response when someone is exposed to Twitter for the first time. "And I need to be on this time-wasting site ... why?"

I don't blame you for wondering. So let me explain it this way: Consider the cell phone. Would you agree that a lot of people use cell phones for idle, mindless chatter? (Insert your own personal teenager reference here.) Of course they do. But does that mean that cell phones are never used for constructive purposes?

Can you think of a time when you used a cell phone to close a business deal or simply get directions or reach someone with important, timely information? I'm sure you can.

Think of Twitter (and all of these new online tools) in the same light. No doubt, many people will use them for nonsensical purposes. But a lot of smart people (including authors and publishers) have figured out ways to leverage them for maximum personal and business advantage.

Consider the restaurant in Buffalo, NY, that uses

Twitter to announce its daily special to everyone who subscribes to its feed. Now that's useful. The web site Mashable.com sends a headline and link for each of its new blog posts. That's smart.

How could an author or book publisher make the best use of Twitter? Let's say you publish books on how to make pancakes. How about a ...

- Pancake recipe of the day
- Reader recipe of the week
- This day in pancake history
- Syrup review of the week

Authors should also use Twitter to alert fans about live workshops and book signings, new chapter samples, new blog posts, media coverage, where their books can be purchased, and more.

A Word of Warning

While I encourage you to be strategic with your Twitter and other social networking activities, I also want to caution you against coming across as too sales-oriented. If all you ever do is post promotional announcements, your followers will tune you out. And that's where injecting some of your personal life can be a good thing.

No, I don't need to know what you have for lunch every day. But if you discover a great new restaurant, that might be worth tweeting about. I don't need to know that you can't sleep and are bored. But you can present it along with a meaningful question, like "Having trouble sleeping. What's your best cure for insomnia?" It's all about finding a balance between useful information, subtle self-promotion, and insightful peeks into your life and personality.

While you can't squeeze a lot of information into those 140 characters, you can and should use Twitter to send your followers to sites and resources throughout the Internet.

Here's a quick list of links that an author might tweet about:

- Links to new articles or blog posts written by you, along with the title or a verbal teaser

- Links to articles or blog posts not written by you that might be of interest to your readers

- Links to instant photos you post from your cell phone using a free service like Twitpic.com

- Links to new video or audio content you post online

- Links to your favorite songs using a web site like Song.ly

Tip: Many links will be too long to fit into your short tweets. In such cases, use a free URL shortener site such as Bit.ly or Tinyurl.com.

Here are seven more Twitter topic ideas with examples of actual tweets I've posted:

- **Requests for help to solve a problem**: "I need to improve how I manage my time. What tools do YOU use to set priorities and get things done?"

- **Questions to stimulate conversation**: "On a scale from 1 to 10, where are you operating today? And why?"

154

- **Quick tips and observations**: "Love the new Task box in Gmail. Got a lot done using it this week. But ... it's not the tool, it's your personal focus that matters!"

- **Teasers about upcoming projects**: "Editing a new podcast — my interview with Dan Kimpel. Should be posted soon."

- **Tweets about unusual personal experiences**: "Just obliterated 2 hornets nests under the table on our deck (got stung 4 times last week). It had to be done."

- **Inspiring quotes**: "I couldn't wait for success, so I went ahead without it." -Jonathan Winters

- **Personal updates that reinforce credibility**: "Just had a great chat session with my Berklee music marketing students."

This isn't spleen surgery. It's just making smart use of new technology. With so many people jumping on the Twitter wagon, it makes sense for you to be there too. So hop on board and start giving your followers tidbits of info they can use — while cementing your reputation as an informative and interesting author.

#50
Post Your Pics on Flickr and Other Photo Sharing Sites

With all the interactive capabilities on the Web these days, digital still photos may seem quite "old school." But don't dismiss the power of your pictures and the opportunity that photo-sharing sites offer to increase your online presence.

Remember that "multiple tentacles" concept we covered in the first part of the book? It's important to leave a trace of yourself and your message in many places where lots of people are gathering online. While YouTube, Facebook and Twitter may grab more headlines, there are many millions of people who still actively surf the photo sites. Therefore, you should be there.

Here are three reasons to post your pictures on photo-sharing sites:

- **Enhance your credibility**. Images show you in action doing what you do. Yes, your book should speak for itself, but offering visual images that your fans and supporters can enjoy adds another layer of credibility to your career. But you must be strategic in how you do this.

  So, post photos of you on the stage, at the computer, and on the road. If you write about plants, show yourself getting your hands dirty in the garden. If you publish a cookbook, display

I use Flickr.com to post photos of me with my favorite people, as well as show book covers, screen shots, and more.

shots of you in the kitchen. Capture the interesting things you encounter along your book publishing journey and share them with others online.

- **Expand your reach.** These photo sites obviously give you a place to upload and store your digital pictures. That means, if you want to use them on your blog or web site, you can simply link to your images on the hosting site instead of messing with uploading them to your own web server.

  More importantly, most of these sites give you badges, widgets and feeds that allow you to share your photo "stream" on other popular web sites. That means you upload images to one site but can share them across several sites.

- **Connect with authority.** I love attending

conferences and events and meeting people I admire, including celebrities. I've had my picture taken with Alec Baldwin, Jack Canfield, Rev. Michael Beckwith, Tavis Smiley, Dr. Ruth Westheimer, Alan Cohen, and many more. I post these photos online, which adds to my credibility by association. You should do the same.

- **Feature your book cover and more**. In addition to uploading photos of yourself and the people you meet, you can also post images of your books, promotional materials, etc.

I discovered the benefit of this by accident when I uploaded the cover of this very book you are reading to Flickr. Some weeks later, I searched for the title on Google and the book cover's Flickr page came up high in the results. I also uploaded a web page screen shot of one of my books when it hit #1 in the Music Business book category on Amazon. What images display your success? Whatever they are, post them now.

- **Spread more of your link bait**. The key to making the best use of photo sharing sites is giving your images precise titles and descriptions. Load them up with the keywords that your ideal readers may use to find things that interest them online.

For instance, with my book cover image, I didn't simply title it "book cover." I labeled it "55 Ways to Promote & Sell Your Book on the Internet." That's why it came up in a Google search, and that's how it acts as another tentacle that helps people discover me on the Internet.

Hot tip: When it comes to places that host still photos on the Web, Flickr.com is king of the heap. Millions of people post and tag their images on this mega site, which was purchased by Yahoo a few years ago. From animals and architecture to water and weddings, you'll find it here. Flickr has free and paid accounts with different feature levels. It's the main photo site I suggest you invest your time in.

But there are other online image hosting sites you should explore as time allows. Here are three more:

Photobucket
www.photobucket.com

Shutterfly
www.shutterfly.com

Picasa Web Albums
picasaweb.google.com

Bottom line: Your book may be primarily comprised of words. But when it comes to promoting it, don't overlook how you can reinforce your message visually.

#51
Use Tagging and Bookmarking Sites to Generate Web Traffic

There are more people surfing the Web and more stuff available to read, hear and see than ever before. It's a crowded, noisy Internet. So how do people find the things that are most relevant to them? Of course, search sites like Google are one of the most common ways that consumers discover things. But a growing method people are using to filter through the clutter is something called "tagging."

If you've ever used web sites like Flickr, YouTube or Delicious, you may already be familiar with tagging. It takes place when someone posts a new photo, video or favorite link on one of these sites and then gives it a descriptive "tag" — one or more words that describe what it is.

Example: If you publish a picture on Flickr taken during your trip to the Grand Canyon, you might give it tags such as "Grand Canyon, Arizona, vacation, hiking."

The important thing about tags on most of these social media sites is this: You aren't the only one who can see and use your tags. Anyone who visits Flickr can search the entire site for photos tagged "Grand Canyon" or "hiking."

And you can quickly find out who else is posting Grand Canyon photos too. This allows you to find other people with similar interests and for them to find you. It's targeted interaction on an extremely personal level.

Using Bookmarking Sites to Promote Your Book

A related trend is referred to as "bookmarking." In essence, bookmarking web sites exist to give people a public place to log and share their favorite links. And guess what? Most of these sites ask users to "tag" their links with descriptive words and phrases too. Which makes these sites great places to find your ideal readers and for them to find you.

When it comes to the bookmarking realm, here are the two most prominent sites:

Delicious
www.delicious.com

Founded in 2003, Delicious is considered one of the first major social bookmarking services. It allows users to tag, save, share and discover web pages from a centralized source. The site has more than five million users and 150 million bookmarked URLs.

StumbleUpon
www.stumbleupon.com

This prominent site is an Internet community of nearly 8 million people that allows its users to discover and rate web pages, photos, and videos. According to the site, "As you click Stumble!, we deliver high-quality pages matched to your personal preferences. These pages have been explicitly recommended by your friends or one of 7 million+ other web surfers with interests similar to you."

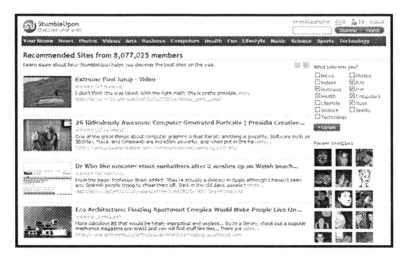

StumbleUpon.com is a prominent bookmarking site that allows its users to discover and rate web pages, photos, and videos.

Hopefully, you understand the potential power of tapping into these existing online communities. While Delicious and StumbleUpon are considered the two main sites in the bookmarking category, there are others, such as:

Diigo
www.diigo.com

Clipmarks
www.clipmarks.com

eSnips
www.esnips.com

Also Consider the Social News Sites

There's another breed of bookmarking site that is focused more on news-related links. Here are six of them:

Digg

www.digg.com

Newsvine

www.newsvine.com

Mixx

www.mixx.com

Propeller

www.propeller.com

reddit

www.reddit.com

Yahoo! Buzz

buzz.yahoo.com

Tagging Revisited

It's one thing to "bookmark" a favorite link on one of these sites. But it doesn't become useful to you or the community until it is "tagged." This is how Delicious defines what a tag is:

"A tag is simply a word you can use to describe a bookmark. Unlike folders, you make up tags when you need them and you can use as many as you like. The result is a better way to organize your bookmarks and a great way to discover interesting things on the Web."

Key lesson: The best way to use tagging to promote your book is to think about the words that fans of your genre or topic use most when searching for stuff online. Then make sure you bookmark lots of links that would be of interest to your readers, and tag them accordingly.

For example, when bookmarking a link to a helpful music marketing article, I tag it with a variety of words and phrases: music marketing, music promotion, band promotion, music sales, promote my music, etc. I think about the words that my idea fans might use to search for this type of information. By including a variety of word combinations in my tags, I increase the likelihood that the right reader will connect with me.

The same goes for links I recommend related to book promotion. Those tags might include: book marketing, book promotion, book sales, promote my book, etc. The more descriptive my tags, the greater the odds that self-promoting authors will find me.

Does this make sense?

Great. Then get busy using bookmarking and tagging to reach even more of your ideal fans online!

#52

Publish Your Own Blog to Engage Readers and Help Search Engines Find You

If you consider yourself a writer, in addition to being an author or book publisher, then I highly recommend you create a blog and add new content to it on a weekly basis.

In an earlier section I covered what blogs are and how they work. So I won't go over those basics here. But what I will emphasize is this: Even if you make use of other people's blogs to promote your book online, you really should publish your own blog as well.

Why? Here are seven things a blog can help you accomplish:

- **Develop a following**. When you create new content on a regular basis, you give readers a reason to reconnect with you and your topic time and time again. A static web site gives no incentives for repeat exposures.

- **Create more tentacles**. You know by now that Internet book marketing is all about outreach and creating a trail of topic-specific breadcrumbs that leads readers to your web site. Every time you publish a new post to your blog, you create yet another trail that your ideal fans can find.

- **Earn better search result positions**. Google and other search engines love blogs because it gives them more content to categorize, and it demonstrates which sites are active and growing. The more active and relevant your blog is, the greater your chances of ranking higher in Google search results.

- **Hone your craft**. Despite your work ethic or best intentions, you never "arrive" at being a great writer. It's a lifelong process that requires constant practice. What better way to motivate yourself to ply your craft and write something every week?

- **Produce material for future books**. I love this aspect of blogs in particular! While you're honing your craft every week, you are also stockpiling a small library of content. And that content can some day be repurposed into articles, reports, white papers, and even new books.

- **Know your industry**. This is especially true for non-fiction authors. If you position your blog as a resource on your topic (which you should), that forces you to always be on the lookout for news, trends, and fresh ideas related to your subject matter. That makes you even more of an expert and the go-to man or woman in your field.

- **Create interaction and community with your readers**. Most bloggers allow readers to leave comments. That's another thing that sets blogs apart from static web pages: people can interact with them. You should encourage and ask your readers to leave comments. That will make your blog a place readers want to visit often and express themselves at while there.

How to Publish Your Own Blog

The great news about blogs: There are many services out there that make it easy to publish one. Here are three popular services to consider:

Blogger
www.blogger.com

A free service owned by Google. Very easy to set up and use. Just choose a template and go.

WordPress
www.wordpress.org and www.wordpress.com

A popular open-source blogging platform that has grown tremendously in recent years. Offers both free and paid versions.

Six Apart
www.sixapart.com

A company that offers multiple free and paid online journal options, including TypePad, Moveable Type, and Vox.

Hot tip: FeedBurner.com is a free service that can help you streamline your RSS feed subscriptions, add interactivity, and include lots of cool features. Use it in combination with one of the blog services above.

Using Your Own Blog to Promote and Sell Books

If you already publish a blog or are about to start one, congratulations! You're miles ahead of many other authors. Now here are several ways you can turn your blog into an online book marketing machine:

- **Deliver your news, your way**. The most basic thing you can do with an author blog is announce your activities: events you're going to attend, new titles you've released, awards you've won, media coverage you've just landed, etc. Let people know about all of your book-related activities. But there are other things you should do with your blog too. So read on ...

- **Share your journey**. A blog can be part personal diary, part "making of" documentary. Invite fans to follow along as you log reports about your adventures through the writing and publishing world. Post daily dispatches from the road, keep fans updated on your creative process, or tell them about the great workshop you gave the night before. Share yourself with your fans and they'll feel more of a connection with you.

- **Post often**. Some bloggers publish something every day; others post entries once or twice a week. Choose a frequency that works for you and do your best to stick with it. I suggest at least one post a week; more if you can swing it. What you want to avoid is DBS (Dead Blog Syndrome) — where weeks or months go by between posts. Lifeless blogs don't get read ... and won't help you sell books!

- **Report on your topic**. Here's an idea that could bring you a lot of targeted traffic. Instead of publishing a blog that promotes you and your book only, create one that acts as a one-stop resource for your entire topic.

For example, if you publish books on stress-free

168

Bob Baker's Full-Time Author Blog

How Publishers Can Succeed Online Where Others Failed

With all the mistakes and radical changes that have taken (and are taking) place in the music industry, where is the book publishing world headed? How will emerging digital technologies continue to impact authors and publishers at all levels?

Those are the ideas discussed in this awesome audio, recorded in New York a couple of months ago at Book Expo during a panel called "Jumping Off a Cliff: How Publishers Can Succeed Online Where Others Failed."

Ideally, your blog should feature attention-getting headlines and images, as well as links to more info about you and your books.

parenting, start the Stress-Free Family Fun Blog. Publish reviews and links to your favorite parenting web sites, books, and organizations. You'll attract a lot of incoming traffic from people searching for solutions to their parenting problems. Of course, you can include plenty of plugs for your own book, but the main focus of the blog will not be on you alone.

• **Extend link love.** There's a lot of cross-referencing that takes place in the blog world. As I mentioned in the previous point, you should regularly scour the Web for news and online resources that would be of interest to your fans. Then write about (and link to) those other blogs, sites, authors, etc.

169

After you publish a new post, send a quick email to the person whose site you plugged. This will often lead to a return link when that webmaster or blogger writes about the exposure they got on your blog. The best way to get link love is to give it unconditionally in the first place.

- **Make your blog post titles sizzle.** Compare the titles you give your blog posts to the headlines that appear on magazine covers. How do they rate? What's more likely to get one of your readers to click a link to read your latest entry: "Some Good Advice" or "7 Things Every Parent Should Know About Cell Phones"? A great title will attract the ideal type of person it's meant for. So take some time to craft the best, attention-grabbing titles you can.

- **Promote new books as you write them.** Instead of waiting for your new book to be published, you can start marketing a new title the day you decide to write it. For nearly two years, author Chris Anderson blogged about the ideas he was researching for his book *The Long Tail*. Doing so gave him valuable feedback he ended up including in the book (which helped him craft a better book) while also creating a buzz and demand for it.

We've only scratched the surface of how to use your own blog to promote and sell more books. But if you take the steps outlined on these pages, you'll have a great headstart in the blog world.

#53
Create Your Own Podcast and Audio Content to Make Connections and Sell Books

If you have any doubts about the effective use of audio to promote books online, just ask Scott Sigler. Since 2005, he's offered all of his horror and science fiction novels as free spoken-word podcast installments. The podcasts for his first novel, *Earthcore*, attracted thousands of subscribers and listeners.

"The free podcasts created an audience for me, which lead to a major five-book deal with Crown Publishing," Sigler says. The first book in that deal, *Infected*, was published in April 2008 and is now being made into a movie by Rogue Pictures. His second novel, *Contagious*, was published in December 2008 and quickly hit the *New York Times* hardcover fiction bestseller list.

"The deal came because I had built a podcast audience by giving away everything I write, unabridged, and in full. No shortcuts, no previews. It's up to the audience to listen to the story and see if they like it enough to buy a print book."

Apparently, readers liked it a lot. Sigler's second podcast novel, called *Ancestor*, had over 30,000 listeners. "I even gave away a free PDF ebook version that was downloaded over 40,000 times." The result of this generosity: When *Ancestor* came out in print in 2007, it hit #2 overall on Amazon.com's fiction list.

The only thing to beat it? A *Harry Potter* novel.

How to Produce Your Own Podcast

Have you dreamed of hosting your own radio show? Many authors have. It's an alluring idea. But ...

Reality check: Just know that a podcast takes more technical skills to publish than a simple text-based blog. You must be familiar with microphones, audio editing software, bit rates, etc. Plus, to be effective with it and build an audience, you'll need to continually produce shows on a regular schedule. The first few are often easy to crank out. But can you sustain that enthusiasm over the long haul?

However, if spoken word audio is your calling, and you can swing it, podcasting offers another great way to interact and share yourself with fans.

The first step is to learn the technical requirements of recording, editing, uploading, and promoting your show. I won't go into all those details here, but I will direct you to these two helpful resources that will shed light on podcasting:

How to Podcast Tutorial
www.how-to-podcast-tutorial.com

How to Create a Podcast
www.youtube.com/watch?v=-hrBbczS9I0

As podcasting has grown, so have the number of services available to help you host and manage your audio files. Here are five podcasting sites that offer a range of free and paid service options:

Blog Talk Radio
www.blogtalkradio.com

Podbean
www.podbean.com

Libsyn
www.libsyn.com

Audio Acrobat
www.audioacrobat.com

Gcast
www.gcast.com

Adding Promotional Punch to Your Podcasts

Here are some ideas on how to use your podcast to promote and sell more books:

- **Do chapter readings.** Probably the easiest podcast format for authors is to do what Scott Sigler did: Read and record the chapters of your books, and release them one by one over time. If you're not comfortable giving away the entire book this way in audio format, then just release a sampling of chapters to whet listener's appetites. Ideally, you should have a pleasing speaking voice to go this route. If not, you could bring on someone to do the readings for you.

- **Share your live events and workshops.** Beyond the content of your book, what else could you offer in audio format? Well, if you started recording all of your workshops, classes and public appearances, you might have a lot of potential material to share. Depending on the length of your live events, you may need to sift through the recordings and only publish the highlights of each one. But this is a great way to create a backlog of audio material.

- **Become a resource**. Author podcasts shouldn't be all about books. But they should focus on your topic in a way that only you as the author can articulate. Look over the tips I offered earlier on using your own blog — especially the "Share your journey" and "Report on your topic" sections. Consider doing spoken-word versions of these. Each episode could feature you talking about your latest experiences or personal take on a current topic. The possibilities are limited only by your imagination.

- **Use an interview format**. Ask a friend or a journalist to do an audio interview with you. Or you can play interviewer and invite other authors and experts to be your guest. Record interviews in person when you attend events or long distance over the phone. Conversations are often more interesting than a solitary voice.

  Tricia Ryan did an audio interview series called "Wednesday Minute Tip of the Week" to promote her book, *Hungry to Succeed?* "The interview was available worldwide and I had immediate sales," she reports. "All these activities helped and were a bit out of the norm."

- **Write attention-getting show titles**. Make sure the name you give each episode is riveting and filled with rich keywords. I'm not talking about how you describe it on the recording. I'm referring to the headline you use on the episode's podcast web page. For example, "What a Week It's Been" is not a strong headline. "How

I Ended Up in Handcuffs in the Back of a Police Car" would grab a lot more attention. Be specific, mysterious, outrageous or funny with your titles ... just don't be dull.

- **Edit your ID3 tags**. These tags supply the information in an MP3 file that is displayed when your audio is played on an iPod or other digital media player. The most important tags are Title, Artist and Album. Don't leave these blank. You want people to know what they're listening to long after they've downloaded your podcast episode. (A free Windows program that can help you do this is MP3tag at www.mp3tag.de/en.)

If your show is called the Radical Relationship Podcast, your Title tag should be something like "RRP 10 - Warning Signs That Your Spouse May Be Cheating On You." Include a standard abbreviation and show number, followed by the episode title.

For the Artist tag, put your name and web site: "Steve Rooney - SteveRooney.com." In the Album tag slot, spell out the full name of the podcast. Taking these steps will ensure that fans are able to store and find your files quickly, and they can get in touch with you when they want.

Think Beyond the Podcast

Keep in mind that podcasts are only one way to use audio content to promote and sell books online. Many authors embed recorded messages onto their web pages using a service such as Audio Acrobat (at bobmsrg.audioacrobat.com). These audio clips can take many forms, including:

175

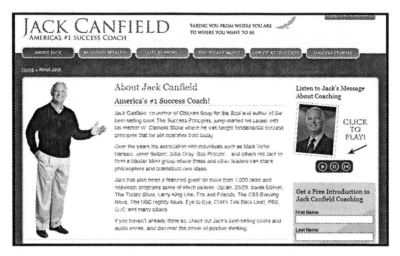

You can also use audio as another way to speak with your web visitors, as Jack Canfield does on this coaching page.

- **Welcome messages.** Greet your web site visitors with an audio message that reinforces what you do and how the site can help them.

- **Testimonials.** Create a call-in line for your readers to leave comments and rave about your book. Then post the best, most flattering audio reviews.

- **Calls to action.** Come right out and tell visitors what you want them to do (place an order, subscribe to your ezine, register for an event) and why they should do it.

No doubt about it: Audio offers a powerful way to promote and sell books online!

#54
Use Video to Spread the Word on YouTube and Beyond

Now that we've covered audio content and reaching readers through their ears, let's jump into video and how to communicate through their eyes. In the same way that there are myriad ways to use spoken-word content, there are also countless ways to incorporate video into your online book promotion plans.

History lesson: At first, the Internet was primarily a text-based medium. Then high-speed access, along with the MP3 and streaming Flash formats, made audio commonplace online. It was only a matter of time before video caught up. And has it ever.

While Internet video doesn't yet match the numbers of broadcast and cable TV viewers, just know that there are many millions of people around the world watching millions of videos online. And they're viewing them increasingly on their cell phones, as well as their regular computers.

This is a growing trend you should definitely embrace. But I recommend you do it not simply because you can, but because using video is yet another way to engage your audience and communicate who you are and what you offer as an author.

Enter the YouTube Kingdom

There are now an endless number of video sites across the Web, but the granddaddy of them all is YouTube.com, which at last count was serving up some 100 million videos a day to its users.

How it works: Once you register for a free YouTube account, you can upload video clips of 10 minutes or less in a variety of formats. The site then converts them to a streaming format that people can view on the YouTube site itself or embedded on other web sites. There's a lot of competition for attention on YouTube, but some videos rise to the top and are seen by millions of people.

While YouTube is the king, there are many other video hosting and sharing sites where you can upload your videos, including these:

Blip.tv
www.blip.tv

Vimeo
www.vimeo.com

Revver
www.revver.com

Dailymotion
www.dailymotion.com

Joost
www.joost.com

Regardless of which site you choose to use, here are six ways to make the most of online video:

- **Don't let a low budget stop you**. If you're

178

sweating because you think your video content has to be a big-budget extravaganza, slap some cold water on your face right now. In this modern era, it's more about the idea behind the visuals than it is the production quality.

Granted, it helps to have a nice camera and editing software (and the skills to use them tastefully). But many people have received widespread exposure using only a $50 webcam on their home computer.

- **Think outside the format box**. On YouTube and other similar sites, videos come in many different forms. They can be as simple as single-camera shots of you speaking in your living room or on a stage, or as complex as documentaries or slick promotional "book trailers."

  But I encourage you to think low budget at first. Record interviews with other experts you meet at conferences, shoot footage of life on the road, or capture the interactions you have with your fans. As long as you're sharing some part of yourself with your readers, it's all fair game.

- **Develop your profile page**. YouTube allows you to design a profile page that contains links to all of your videos, a short bio, and a link to your personal web site. Also, people can subscribe to your "channel" and get updates whenever you post new video content. You want to encourage this connection. And while you're at it, subscribe to and leave comments on other video producers' work, which will cause your name to appear on their pages.

- **Elicit a strong reaction for maximum effect**. There are no sure-fire recipes for creating a popular viral video. But I have noticed that the most-viewed online videos have some common traits. The main element they share: inspiring a physical or emotional response from viewers.

  In other words, if you can get someone to laugh or cry or be moved in some meaningful way by a video clip, you increase the chances that he or she will tell someone else about it. So think about the emotional impact you can add to your videos before you create them.

- **Keep them short**. People are busy. Attention spans are getting shorter as Web surfers learn to quickly scan and filter out what they will and won't spend time on. You might be tempted to treat people to your 10-minute magnum opus on growing geraniums. But it would be much better for your viewers if you broke it up into three separate videos. In fact, I recommend you try to keep your online videos to no more them three minutes each.

- **Embed videos on your own site with a purpose**. While you want your videos to be found on YouTube and other video sites, you should also create clips to be used primarily on your web site. Remember the discussion of audio greetings in the previous section? You can use videos in the same way: welcome messages on your home page, calls to action on your ezine sign-up page, a testimonials reel of raving fans on your sales page, and more.

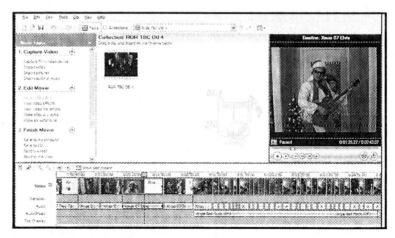

Windows Movie Maker is a powerful little free video editing program that comes installed on most PCs.

Editing tip: Most computers come with free video editing software these days. If you have a PC, look for Windows Movie Maker. If you work on a Mac, you may have a free copy of iMovie.

Uploading tip: Since uploading large video files can take a bit of time, most people don't want to mess with starting accounts at multiple video sharing sites. However, you should be aware of TubeMogul.com, a site that will upload your videos to several popular sites at the same time.

The Newest Trend: Live Streaming Video

You may have noticed that the digital world we live in is feeding the human need for instant gratification. We want information, music, books, movies, and games ... and we want them now! And more increasingly, we can get what we want online right away. Hence, the instant download.

In the video world, the latest extension of that

trend is the ability to stream video live — as it happens. No waiting to shoot, convert, edit and upload the file. Just hook up your webcam and log on to one of the free streaming video sites, and you're ready to broadcast live to the world — as long as you can attract an audience.

There are many ways authors can use this technology, such as: hold live virtual workshops, present question and answer sessions, give chapter readings, do live demonstrations, etc.

Here are four of the top streaming video sites:

Ustream.tv
www.ustream.tv

Stickam
www.stickam.com

LiveVideo
www.livevideo.com

Qik
www.qik.com

As you can see, there are countless ways to employ video in your online book promotion efforts. So pick an idea, grab a camera, and become your own instant indie film producer.

55

Consider LinkedIn, Squidoo, MySpace, Ning, and Other Social Networking Sites

We've already covered a wide variety of tools, web sites, and services you can use to launch your own Internet book promotion campaign. In this final section, I give you a final rundown of several other sites you should be aware of as you plan your online book awareness strategy.

- **LinkedIn.com** — A prominent social site for professional networking. Be sure to tap into the Groups and Questions features, as well as the ReadingList by Amazon application.

- **Squidoo.com** — A popular publishing platform and community that makes it easy to create "lenses," which are pages that gather everything you know about a topic of interest. Squidoo offers a great way to establish yourself as an expert in your field.

- **MySpace.com** — You've no doubt heard of this one. It's been losing steam in recent years, but if your book caters to a younger audience and is related to music and entertainment, you should have a presence on MySpace. Be sure to post bulletins and events there.

- **Ning.com** — This popular site, which boasts nearly 30 million members, gives you the ability to create your own social networking site on the topic of your choice — complete with discussion forums and video, audio and photo upload capabilities.

- **CraigsList.org** — This is the free announcement web site that made the traditional newspaper classified ad section obsolete. Use Craig's List to promote your events, services, and more. Just be sure to look over the site's posting policies first.

- **FriendFeed.com** — A great service that makes it easy to funnel all of your various online RSS feed activity (blog posts, Twitter, photos, video, audio, and more) into one place. Check out the widgets there too.

- **Google Wave** (at wave.google.com) — As I was going to press with this book, Google was about to release a new service called Google Wave, described as "equal parts conversation and document. People can communicate and work together with richly formatted text, photos, videos, maps, and more." This potentially could become big, so look into it.

- **Meetup.com** — This site's mission is to "revitalize local community and help people around the world self-organize." Meetup makes it easy for anyone to organize a local group or find one of thousands already meeting face-to-face.

- **Friendster.com** — One of the first social networking sites, Friendster has more than 100 million members worldwide. Like many others these days, the site helps people stay in touch

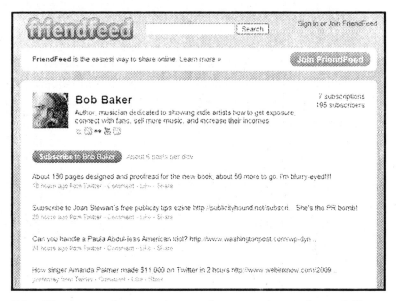

FriendFeed.com allows you to compile your various online activities (blog posts, Twitter, photos, video, audio, and more) into one feed.

with friends and discover new people and things that are important to them.

- **Tagged.com** — This site claims to be the third largest social network in the US with more than 80 million members worldwide. I haven't used it thus far, but it might be worth a peek.

- **Skype.com** — Use this service to make free phone calls and even video chat sessions with friends and customers. Some authors offer Skype consulting and coaching sessions for a fee.

- **Hi5.com** — Launched in 2003, hi5 is yet another well traveled social network with over 60 million unique monthly visitors.

- **Bebo.com** — A site that "combines community, self-expression and entertainment, enabling you to consume, create, discover, curate and share digital content in entirely new ways."

- **Plaxo.com** — This one started as an online address book service, but has branched out into a more robust networking site that encourages interaction between members.

It was tough limiting this book to just 55 ways to promote and sell your book online. I could have easily reached the ever-popular "101 ways" plateau. But I had to end it somewhere, and I didn't want to overburden you with too many choices. (I know, I probably crossed the overburden threshold somewhere around the 29th way.)

But you get the picture: There are seemingly countless ways to use the Internet to make money (and make a difference) as an author and book publisher. I've done my best to give you my top tips and strategies on this topic. And I sincerely hope you now feel more educated and better equipped to take your message to the people online.

Before you dive in, please turn the page and read my final thoughts as I encourage you to take the "*55 Ways* Internet Book Promotion Challenge"!

The "55 Ways" Internet Book Promotion Challenge

"The best way to succeed at anything is to develop a community around your talents and expertise."

The phrase above is adapted from a slogan used by Scott Flora, president of the Small Publishers Association of North America (SPAN). I think it sums up my best advice on how to approach Internet book promotion and make it work for you.

Here's just one example of this concept in action:

In the spring of 2009, speaker and novelist Andy Andrews released *The Noticer*, a book that encourages readers to recognize the five people who have had the biggest impact on their lives. Instead of relying on the traditional marketing avenues to reach consumers, he created an online campaign called The Noticer Project.

He started a Facebook group and a Twitter account dedicated to the topic, he posted videos about it on YouTube, and created a web site at TheNoticer Project.com. Then he encouraged people to publicly "notice" the five most influential people in their lives. The web site also includes instructions on how to do it: make a phone call, send an email, publish a blog post, interact via the Facebook group, send a tweet, etc.

This is a great example of how to use the social and interactive aspects of the Web for smart book promotion. Andrews and his publisher aren't just shouting, "Hey, I have a new book out! Buy it!"

Key: Instead, they are encouraging people to actively engage in the message of the book. By doing so, they make a deeper connection with potential readers and create awareness of the book as a byproduct of a bigger mission.

You should take a similar approach with your book promotion!

Internet marketing, when done effectively, isn't about using online tools to simply interrupt people so you can stand out in a crowded marketplace. The real purpose is to engage people and draw them into your world; to create a spirit of community around your ideas and personality.

My Challenge to You

Now that you've read this book and have absorbed all 55 ways, I want you to start putting these tactics into action. Then, let me know the successes and challenges you experience while implementing them. And I'm going to give you some great ways to do that, while also sharing your book promotion journey with other self-promoting authors and readers of this book.

But first, the challenge ...

In the next 7 days ...

Pick at least three ideas from the book and implement them right away. Strike while your interest and resolve are high. Take action now! Treat yourself to some mini successes in the short term to fuel your motivation for the long term.

Steps you can take in the next week include:

- **Start a free ezine** (if you don't offer one already). Sign up for one of the email management services and get familiar with sign-up forms, delivery options, etc.

- **Beef up your personal author web site** (or start one, if you don't yet have a site). Look over the web site chapters and tweak the design and text so it attracts your ideal readers and buyers.

- **Set aside time every day or two to read blogs, listen to podcasts, and watch video clips.** Become an informed consumer of these formats so you have a better idea of how to use them yourself for promotion.

Here are more steps you can potentially take in the weeks and months ahead:

In the next 30 days ...

- **Start a blog**, if you don't already publish one. Go to either Blogger.com or Wordpress.org and start a free account. Then get busy posting something new every week.

- **Open free accounts on Facebook.com and Twitter.com.** Spend time filling out the various sections of your profile so people know who you are, what you look like, and what you do.

- **Make sure the ordering process is clear on your web site.** Do you make it easy for people to purchase your book? Include a "call to action."

- **Write and distribute articles and sample chapters** via one or more of the free article sites, such as EzineArticles.com. Also offer your articles to relevant web sites and ezines, as long as they link back to your site.

- **Reach out to bloggers, podcasters, and journalists** who cover your specific genre or field. Compliment them, introduce yourself, and start relationships with them.

In the next 90 days ...

- **Make sure you are staying on top of your previous book promotion activities**: sending email updates to your list, researching your genre or field, blogging every week, updating your status and interacting on Facebook and Twitter (or whatever it is that you set in motion previously).

- **Enroll your book in the Amazon Advantage Program** (if it's not already distributed to Amazon via another source) and complete your Amazon Author Profile page.

- **Spread more "link bait"** by posting your articles and presentations on document sites such as Scribd.com and SlideShare.com.

- **Start free accounts at YouTube.com, Flickr.com, LinkedIn.com, Squidoo.com**, and as many popular social networking sites as time allows. Make the effort to completely fill out your profile pages on each.

In the next six months ...

- **Take time to assess your progress** over the past three months. What has worked for you? What hasn't worked? Why? What can you do better?

- **Start your own podcast** and/or start posting short video clips that promote your message and your book. Encourage people to share the links with their friends.

- **Seek out cross-promotional partnerships** and affiliate arrangements with other web sites, authors, and organizations.

- **Combine your online efforts with your real world activities**. At live events, collect names and email addresses and make people aware of your address on the Web. Use your Web presence and the various event web sites listed earlier to promote your public appearances.

- **Learn more about RSS feeds** and how to cross-pollinate your blog posts, photos, videos, and text updates onto multiple web sites automatically.

- **Keep chipping away at it** and continue to be an evangelist for your topic. Spread your message online by any ethical means necessary.

Now Report Your Progress

Don't promote your book in a vacuum. I want you to share your experiences with me and other authors who are on this same book marketing journey.

Here are the best ways to connect:

191

Subscribe to my free "Full-Time Author" ezine and blog. Just visit FullTimeAuthor.com to find them and sign up. Read the posts and leave comments.

Join my "Internet Book Promotion, Marketing & Sales Strategies" group on Facebook. Introduce yourself to the community, start or respond to a discussion thread, post links to helpful articles, and more.

The Facebook group is located here:

www.facebook.com/group.php?gid=107052554323

Or you can just go to the Groups section on Facebook and search for "Internet Book Promotion, Marketing & Sales." (Make sure I'm listed as the admin.)

I also encourage you to friend and follow me on Facebook and Twitter:

www.facebook.com/BobBaker

www.twitter.com/MrBuzzFactor

And if you are interested in my music marketing sites and want to see how I use the Internet to create a presence on those topics, please visit

www.TheBuzzFactor.com

www.MusicPromotionBlog.com

Other Recommended Action Steps

Here are two organizations you should join that provide invaluable resources:

The Independent Book Publishers Association is a trade organization specifically for independent authors and publishing companies.

Independent Book Publishers Association

www.ibpa-online.org (IBPA, formerly PMA)

Small Publishers Assoc of North America

www.spannet.org

And here are several blogs I recommend you read for ongoing marketing advice:

Bob Baker's Full-Time Author Blog

www.bob-baker.com/self-publish-book/blog

Book Marketing Bestsellers

blog.bookmarket.com

Infoproduct Marketing Insiders

www.highertrustmarketing.com/blog

Plug Your Book
www.weberbooks.com/publish.htm

Published and Profitable
blog.publishedandprofitable.com

Writer's Weekly
www.writersweekly.com

Best Seller Book Marketing
www.bestsellerauthors.com/blog

Author Marketing Experts
www.amarketingexpert.com/ameblog

Hello, My Name Is Blog
hellomynameisscott.blogspot.com

Seth Godin's Blog
sethgodin.typepad.com

You now have an arsenal of Internet book promotion tools at your disposal. Now go forth and put them to use!

There's no denying the opportunities for you to make a splash, make a difference, and make money with your book. And there's no shortage of useful tools at your disposal — many of which are free.

The only question that remains is …

How will you put them to use?

I wish you an abundance of success, and I look forward to hearing about your progress as you successfully promote and sell your book online.

-Bob

Special Recognition Section

When I originally launched this book, I did something unusual — dare I say "revolutionary"? I starting selling access to the book's content as I was writing it. That's right, months before the book was completely written, designed and printed ... I started pre-selling it.

Many independent musicians have used this "fan funding" method before, but it was practically unheard of in the book publishing world. I encourage you to expand your thinking in the same way and consider new ways you can write, produce, promote, and share what you create.

I want to thank the following people who were brave enough to take me up on my pre-publication offer. I applaud and recognize them for playing an important role in the success of this book!

Ian Narcisi, www.IanMusic.com
Independent musician: singer/songwriter, drummer, keyboardist. Progressive rock that speaks to your soul!

DLUX the Light, www.DluxTheLight.com
Performing artist and producer of the most enlightening spoken-word hip-hop to entertain your soul!

Bobbye Middendorf, www.WriteSynergiesCopywriting.com
Bringing heart to marketing copy, content & coaching for Conscious Creators: Express your gifts and greatness. Connect w/ clients. Succeed!

Dada Nabhaniilananda, www.EternalWave.com
Musician, yoga monk & meditation teacher. Author of *Close Your Eyes & Open Your Mind: An Introduction to Spiritual Meditation*.

Luke Hudson aka Netvalar, www.TimelineOnline.org
Record Label 2.0 I believe is the building up of options for music lovers to fully participate in the music industry.

Ronnie Mason, www.RonnieMason.com
A classic country music recording artist reminiscent of Marty Robbins with the vocal range of Roy Orbison. Hear song clips at the web site.

Vikki Flawith, www.VikkiFlawith.com
Champion of the creatively introverted, Amazon of the socially terrified, opera-howling blogger, and Aquarian cyber-geek extraordinaire.

K6artlessonplans.com, www.k6artlessonplans.com
Quick and easy K-6 art lesson plans matched to national standards for art teachers, regular education teachers, and homeschoolers!

Steve Marconi, books.trafford.com/07-2949
Author of *Amazing UFO Sightings in the Hudson Valley, Hidden Technology & the Coming Great Deception*, a book about earth-based UFOs.

Dave Jackson, www.MusiciansCooler.com
A podcast featuring tips on getting more gigs, fans, and music sales. The Musicians Cooler is "where musicians come to trade advice."

Debra Russell, www.Artists-Edge.com
Business coach, trainer & speaker in the arts and entertainment industry. Empowering you to make a prosperous living doing what you love.

Bonnie Lavine, author of *6,000 Milestones*, a memoir of one woman's soul-searching and healing while traveling alone in the deserts of the Southwest USA.

Walter Hanson, www.HansonMusicStudios.com
Online guitar and piano lessons. Webcam music production. Get your song produced at reasonable rates.

Dave Richardson, www.VnRescues.com
Author of *Vietnam Air Rescues*. Experience the heart-pounding action of a rescue pilot. See and feel what it was really like to save a life.

Michelle Gold, www.MichelleGold.com

Phoenix Imagery Press, LLC, www.PhoenixImageryPress.com
Publisher of *America's Road* & *Among These Hallowed Grounds*.
Photographers/writers specializing in the Eastern US to the
Mississippi.

Gregory Victor Babic, www.GregBabic.com
This Australian author has entered the American fiction market with
two novels just released by AllThingsThatMatterPress.com.

Christian Calcatelli, www.Solo-Piano.com
Classical piano music for the MTV generation. Dangerously
emotional, wildly energizing, vividly inspiring!

Cynthia Morse, www.VirtuallyAtYourService.biz
Virtual assistant specializing in work with authors. Take your business to the next level by allowing me to handle the details for you.

Kathleen Palmer

Heather Anderson, www.thesosj.com
The Story of Sadie Jones: An illustrated musical storybook about a
girl named Sadie, brought to life by musicians from around the
world.

Blue Rabbit, www.BlueRabbitMusic.com
Alternative indie-pop for artful lyric lovers w/ out-of-the-box tastes.
Haunting melodies in 3-part harmony over drums, cello & Celtic
harp.

Alice Vedral Rivera, www.myspace.com/alicevrivera
Poet and author of *Dearest and Most Precious: A Love Journal*. A
look inside the mind and heart of a passionate woman in love.

Philip Horváth, www.PhilipHorvath.com
Transformational catalyst, counselor, consultant, and founder of
c3: Center for Conscious Creativity.

Blues Jam Central, www.BluesJamCentral.com
Join Blues Jam Central and allow your blues jam players to sign up
on the Internet and get online jam scheduling.

Per Kristian Indrehus, www.CamelonMedia.no

David Stoddard, www.GetOuttaMyWay.com
The Unmotivated Motivational Writer gently nudges you onto a path
where you can't help but "Get Outta Your Own Way."

Ardy Skinner, www.LavishCheapskate.com
Author of *The Lavish Cheapskate*. Everyday strategies to free up
money! Turn hundreds of $$ in savings into thousands!

David Page, MD, www.DavidPageBooks.com
The Phoenix Prescription is an ethics challenge in a novel. An
inspirational story for anyone with a loved one facing extreme
illness.

Cheese Excursion, www.CheeseExcursion.com
Awesome fun-time party band from Australia. Features trumpet,
trombone, saxophone, guitars, drums, and a wall of vocals. Hurrah!

Leonard Patterson, www.DanceFouls.com
Great T-shirts, bad memories. Express yourself, but please dance
responsibly!

Thomas Kobela

Pamela Ruby Russell, www.cdbaby.com/rubytunes
Songwriter/Photographer: Art that inspires & enlivens. *Highway of
Dreams* CD & extraordinary photos avail. Invite her into your heart
now.

Alexis Tapp, www.Jackowhisp.com.au
Author of *Jimba Jackobean and the Bouncer-Bangerrings*. 1st of the
Jack-o-Whisp series of children's picture-books. Released Christmas
2009.

Tracy Cooper-Posey, www.TracyCooperPosey.com
National award-winning romantic suspense author of 19 titles,
winner of the Emma Darcy Award, and owner of the Anchored
Authors blog.

Marc Rosen, www.DancingHippoMusic.com
Cool music, not smooth or crazy bop. Great jazz, perfect for
listening to while writing or any time you need to be inspired by
great tunes!

Charr Crail, www.CharrCrail.com
Author & illustrator of *Faeries in Our Midst*. An extraordinary
collection of stories/photo imagery illuminating the unseen world
of Charr Crail.

Debra Byron, www.myspace.com/davebyronmusic
The book I'm writing is *Start Your Own Music Career*. It will feature step by step how I took Dave Byron's music & turned it into our career.

Louis F. Vargas, author of *The Passion-Driven Life*

Steve Pasek, www.BizWebsites.org
Small-biz web site hosting and Internet marketing consulting. Increase your bottom line with a web site that earns its keep.

Bob Foster, www.BizMaverickBlog.com
Author of *Be Your Own Turnaround Manager: A Common Sense Guide to Managing a Business Crisis*. Manage your biz problems before they're fatal.

Carol Hansen Grey, www.SimpleHealingTools.com
Author of *Simple Healing Tools on the Path to Personal Empowerment and Inner Peace*. Also see OpenHeartPress.com.

Gary W Patterson, www.FiscalDoctor.com
Stick Out Your Balance Sheet and Cough book details proven methods to successfully treat companies of all sizes across a range of industries.

Samuel Odunsi

John Willmott, www.CelticWays.com
Join us in Ireland, explore ancient sites & traditions plus bard school retreat for writing, poetry & harps as we believe everyone is a bard.

Rob Richards
A singer-songwriter from Johannesburg, South Africa.

Douglas Niedt, www.DouglasNiedt.com

Joel D Canfield, www.JoelCanfield.com
Author of the *Commonsense* business books which help humanise your business to develop trusting relationships through better communication.

Lynnette Schuepbach, www.KidsDoRead.com
Author/illustrator of colorful children's picture books for ages 0-7 and stories for ages 6-12, all with tips for parents and teachers.

Bhavani Jampala

Norma Pimenta, www.NormaPimenta.com
Author of *Smiling Eyes, A Cheerleading Coach's Personal Victory*. An inspiring novel of triumph & recovery following a bizarre tragedy.

Lawson Broadrick, www.LawsonBroadrick.com
Author of *That's Just the Way It Was*, a memoir of humorous stories about growing up in a small Southern town during the Great Depression.

Frank Reddon and Lou Anne Reddon, www.Enzepplopedia.com
Authors/editor/publishers of *Sonic Boom: The Impact of Led Zeppelin. Volume 1 – Break & Enter*.

Doug Higgins, www.MontanaBrass.com

Bill T Tucker, www.NoGoinBack.com
Author of *No Goin' Back*. "Be grateful you haven't lived his life. Be inspired by what he acheived." True life story.

Mary D'Amato, www.RxMgt.com

Deborah Diak, www.RisingStarArtists.com
Rising & Mega Star Artists

Toni McMurphy, www.ToniMcMurphy.com
Speaker/coach/facilitator. Inspiring people to bring out the best in themselves and each other while navigating the human side of business.

Michael Meade, www.Lackawannarail.com
Independent singer/songwriter now working on his first (notice the confidence!) book and hoping to pursue self-publishing.

Julie Hood, www.OrganizedWriter.com
Ever wonder how much you could write if you were more organized? Find out w/ the FREE Planner from Julie Hood at OrganizedWriter.com.

Linda Kluge, www.4Secrets4Gamblers.com
Gambling Balance coaching for all who want to "Stay in the Game for Life" using a controlled gambling approach and self-assessment tools.

Ernie J. Zelinski, www.Retirement-Cafe.com
Author of *How to Retire Happy, Wild, and Free* (over 100,000 copies sold) and *The Joy of Not Working* (225,000+ copies sold).

Home Jewelry Business Success Tips
www.JewelryBusinessTips.com
Your guide to a profitable handcrafted jewelry business. Thousands of ideas, strategies and tips for selling your handcrafted jewelry.

Creative Conflict Resolutions, www.CreativeConflicts.com
Solutions and support to resolve abusive marriage and work relationships. Find conflict coaching, ebooks, and articles to heal your life.

Myztery, www.Myztery.net
An alternative rock band with a splash of techno from Vancouver, BC, founded by Diamond and Star.

Corinne Richardson, www.CorinneRichardson.com
Helping people simplify the second half of their lives with home, office & wardrobe consultations and the book *Dressing Nifty After Fifty*.

Do This Right Now and Get Ongoing Inspiration!

You have just embarked on an exciting Internet book promotion adventure. No doubt, there's work to be done and there will be challenges ahead, but the potential rewards that lie before you just may exceed your greatest expectations.

But to enjoy the rewards you must be vigilant in the pursuit of your book publishing goals. You must stay focused and regularly feed your mind with new ideas and fresh perspectives on marketing. That's why I encourage you to think of this book as an important first step in your journey.

I invite you to stay in touch with me and report your progress. So before you get distracted, please visit my web site at **FullTimeAuthor.com** and download a copy of *Self-Publishing Confidential*, a free report filled with my best book publishing and marketing advice. And while you're there, sign up for my free *Full-Time Author* ezine.

Also, send me a friend invite on Facebook at **Facebook.com/BobBaker** and follow me on Twitter at **Twitter.com/MrBuzzFactor**.

Hope to see you online soon.

To your success!

–Bob